VIDEO
IN PHOTOSHOP
FOR **PHOTOGRAPHERS** AND **DESIGNERS**

Video in Photoshop for
Photographers and Designers
ISBN: 9780133375169
CODE: 3798455C504F

Redeem Your Product Code

1. Sign in or create an account at
   www.peachpit.com/account.

2. On the Account page, enter your code in
   the field that appears in the **"Digital
   Product Voucher"** box at the top of the
   right column.

3. Click '**Submit your code**'.

4. The product will be listed under
   Digital Purchases on your Account page.
   Click the **"refresh"** link(s) in order to
   generate your file(s) for download.

Peachpit

PEACHPIT PRESS

LIN SMITH

Video in Photoshop for Photographers and Designers
Colin Smith

Peachpit Press
www.peachpit.com

To report errors, please send a note to errata@peachpit.com

Peachpit is a division of Pearson Education.

Copyright © 2013 Colin Smith

Senior Editor: Karyn Johnson
Developmental Editor: Anne Marie Walker
Production Editor: Katerina Malone
Copy Editor: Kelly Kordes Anton
Proofreader: Liz Welch
Technical Editor: Bruce Bicknell
Composition: WolfsonDesign
Indexer: Jack Lewis
Interior Design: Kim Scott, Bumpy Design
Cover Design: Mimi Heft

ISBN-13: 978-0-321-83456-0
ISBN-10:   0-321-83456-9

9 8 7 6 5 4 3 2 1

ACKNOWLEDGMENTS

This is the most difficult part of the book to write, because I just know I'm going to leave off some very special and important people. So please forgive me now! You know who you are anyway.

A book like this requires a tireless and dedicated team of people to make it happen.

I would like to thank the entire team at Peachpit Press. Thanks to Karyn Johnson for being Wonder Woman and using your magic lasso to round up all the cats to make this come together while working around the clock, and also for your friendship throughout the years. To Anne Marie Walker and Kelly Kordes Anton, thanks for your tireless editing and making me sound good. Shout out to Damon Hampson, Nancy Ruenzel, Ted Waitt, Nancy Davis, Gary-Paul, and the rest of the Peachpit crew in San Fran, too!

I'd like to thank Ernie Schaffer for teaching me the difference between a video editor and just connecting bits of video—plus the late-night music jams. Adrian Ramseier, gratitude for putting up with the endless barrage of questions and the occasional game of chess.

To all my friends at Adobe, I don't even want to start listing off names because I know I'll forget a very important one or two. It's been an honor and a lot of fun working and playing with you guys for all these years.

I also want to thank my fellow instructors, exhibitors, and other friends in the industry —especially the amazingly talented authors we have at PhotoshopCAFE/Software Cinema. You are my *whānau* (extended family). Thanks for keeping me inspired.

To my staff at PhotoshopCAFE, especially Bruce Bicknell and Mike Freze, you guys are the best! Thanks for picking up the slack while I've been busy on this book.

Last and not least, thanks to all the loyal members of PhotoshopCAFE. If it weren't for you, I wouldn't be doing this. See you at the CAFE!

CONTENTS

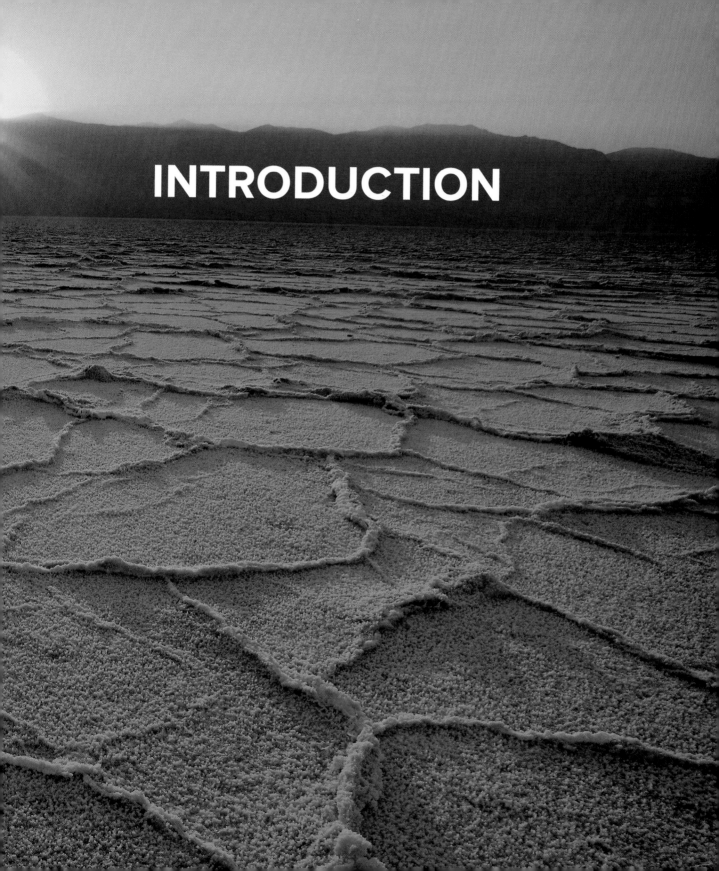

INTRODUCTION

THE OTHER DAY, I was happily munching the last remaining bites of a strip of blackened salmon and enjoying the outdoor sunshine during a Southern California–style lunch. I spun my head to see what the loud squawking sound behind me was all about and noticed two birds fighting over a piece of food. Finally, one feathered fighter puffed out his little chest in victory. Then, the fierce look on his face changed to that of worry and bewilderment, as if to say, "I won the battle, but now what?" You see, the piece of food was larger than this little chap could carry away.

This reminds me of a photographer with a sparkling new HDSLR camera that is capable of shooting stunning HD video. You can see the proud new owner thinking: "I have a great new camera. I have shot the video. Now what? What do I do with it? How can I fix up that video and share it with the world?"

Plenty of information is available on capturing video and shooting in this "HDSLR revolution." But very little has been said about editing the footage. Usually, you just hear people suggesting that budding filmmakers use Adobe Premiere Pro or Apple Final Cut Pro—without regard for the fact that many photographers and designers are unwilling or unable to invest all the time needed to learn and use a professional editing suite. On the other hand, designers and photographers already know and love Photoshop, which can now produce professional quality video-editing results.

That's where this book steps in. The book begins with some basics about shooting video and tips for you to get the best possible footage onto your sensor in the first place. After that, you will learn how to get that footage onto your computer in an organized fashion so that you can find it when you need it. You will learn how to use Adobe Bridge and Adobe Lightroom for these tasks.

The main section of the book walks you through various techniques of editing and cutting your video together in Adobe Photoshop. You'll learn how to edit projects that include working with video, slideshows, interviews, and stacked video with smooth transitions.

The video projects will sound great, too, because you will learn about getting the most out of the audio and even adding backing music tracks. You will even get to dabble in motion graphics and create lower thirds and title screens, and animate video and motion graphics. You won't be left hanging at the end either, where you will learn how to output and render the video so that it can be viewed on mobile devices, laptops, and the Web. Best of all, it's easy and you don't have to have a deep knowledge of video.

Who Should Read This Book

If you are a photographer, designer, or Photoshop enthusiast who captures digital video or has to work with digital video, this book is for you. You may be working with an HDSLR camera, a point-and-shoot camera, or even an iPhone's camera, and that's great. The lessons don't discriminate between the different types of video as the workflows are the same. You don't need prior knowledge of video editing or motion graphics to use this book. Complete beginners and users with a little experience will not be left behind. Meanwhile, experienced Photoshop users will get a lot out of the video and motion graphics workflows presented in these pages.

If you are serious video pro and use applications such as Premiere Pro and Adobe After Effects on a daily basis, you may pick up a few tips—but you aren't really the intended audience for this book or the video features in Adobe Photoshop.

Because of my own real-world experience in photography, video, and motion graphics, I presented the lessons as real-world projects that are typical to the kinds of projects you will work on. You will find no video jargon in these pages that isn't related to photography or explained. This is video editing for photographers and designers—not tech-talking video pros. It's my goal to provide you with the skills and creative jumpstart you need to become inspired and comfortable using Photoshop as your editing tool to edit and produce your own high-quality projects that will make your clients, friends, and family happy.

About the Lesson Files and Resources

To bring the information on these pages to life and provide more information, this book provides a download of resources that include lesson files, sample footage, and videos. Use the lesson files to complete the book's step-by-step tutorials and review the before-and-after samples to check your work. In addition to lessons files and footage, you'll find PhotoshopCAFE video training that explores additional topics.

To download and use these files, you will need the following:

- Adobe Photoshop CS6 or newer. (Extended version not required.)

- A high-speed Internet connection to download the lesson files.

- Speakers or headphones to monitor the audio files on the projects.

To access the download, visit the Peachpit website (peachpit.com), sign in, and register this book (it's all free). To register the book, once you sign in, go to Account, then Registered Products, and click on "Access Bonus Content." Copy the download to any location you prefer on your system. (If necessary, double-click the file to unzip it.) Take a look at the download to see how the chapters, footage, and music folders are organized as you will be accessing these during the tutorials.

Saving and Managing Projects

When working on your video editing projects, it's always a good idea to save your work as you go. But how are projects saved and managed in Photoshop? Files are saved in PSD format as indicated by the .psd file extenion. The PSD contains all the trims edits, text, graphics, and basically everything except the video footage and audio files. The video footage isn't embedded into the PSD as this would make a huge file that might cause problems and limitations to the video length.

Instead of embedding the video, Photoshop PSD files reference the video. This means that you choose a location to save the video files and Photoshop points to the original files when you place them into a project. If you move the original video clips, rename them, or delete them, the links to the references are broken. If you open a project with broken links, the Cannot Locate Missing Media dialog displays (as shown in **FIGURE 0.1**) so you can relink the video. You may need to relink videos when opening project files during these tutorials—and while you work on collaborative projects as well.

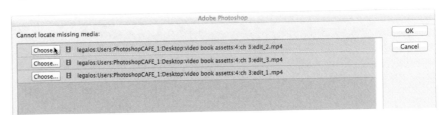

FIGURE 0.1 When you open project files in Photoshop, they are checked for missing media.

To relink the videos, follow these steps:

1. Click the missing footage's Choose button.

2. Navigate to the location of the missing video clip, select it, and click Open (**FIGURE 0.2**).

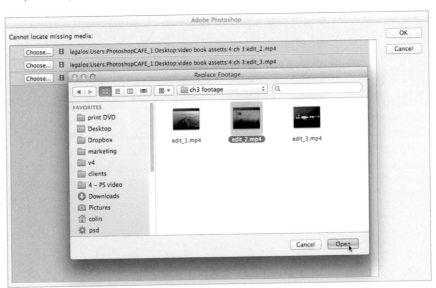

FIGURE 0.2 Relinking the missing footage.

3. Once the footage is relinked, a check box displays to the left of the footage name (**FIGURE 0.3**). If the other missing clips are in the same folder, they will be updated automatically as well. Otherwise, you will need to click the Choose button for each missing footage file and update the links.

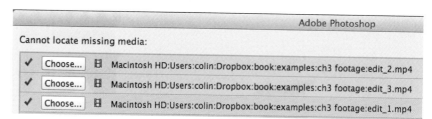

FIGURE 0.3 The relinked and updated footage.

4. When you are finished updating footage, click the OK button to continue onward to work in Photoshop.

CHAPTER 1

SHOOTING VIDEO: THE BASICS OF VIDEO PRODUCTION

IN A SENSE, VIDEO IS JUST LIKE PHOTOGRAPHY. In fact, the principles of exposure, composition, and lighting are the same. A video is nothing more than multiple images. In cinema, 24 images (or frames) are displayed every second; in video, 30 frames are displayed every second. One important aspect to bear in mind is that video, just like good photography, is all about storytelling. I've had the privilege of meeting and interviewing some of the most successful directors and filmmakers in the industry, and storytelling is a constant theme in these discussions. People want to know who the characters are and what will happen.

As photographers, you may already have a basic (or advanced) knowledge of exposure, composition, and other image-making factors, but the big shift in storytelling is that photographers are used to telling the story in a single frame. In this book you'll learn how to capture and edit multiple frames and use the element of time and motion to add to your visual storytelling skills. In this chapter, you'll learn about the basics of lighting, camera setup, and movement. You will also learn about some of the equipment that is currently available to help a photographer or videographer capture the best possible footage.

Shooting Video vs. a Photograph

In video, the element of time needs to be considered. You still need to tell a story, but you no longer need to tell it all in a single frame. When you look at some of the best examples of video, you will see how the setup involves an action or story revealed over time. This technique adds anticipation, holds viewers' attention, and keeps them glued to the screen until the story unfolds. If people watched a feature film for only 10 minutes, that would be a disaster. However, if they gazed at and got lost in a photograph for a full 10 minutes, that would be an accomplishment; hence one of the major differences between video and a still photo.

Compositionally, in a photograph the viewer stares at the image and perhaps over time notices subtle details that aren't immediately obvious. The eye is drawn to the brightest portion or the dominant portion of the photograph. Leading lines draw the eye into a photograph. This is all true for video as well. However, motion trumps all other image elements. The viewer's eye will wander the image, but as soon as there is movement, it will attract the eye immediately, which opens up new creative opportunities.

When you also add the element of sound, you introduce feeling and emotion, as well as a clue to what is happening in the video. To illustrate, try watching a movie with the sound turned off; you'll notice that a lot of the impact has been removed.

Equipment for Great Video

Let's explore the kinds of equipment and techniques that you can use to capture high-quality video.

Cameras

To record video, you can utilize many different types of cameras, ranging from a simple iPhone to a video-enabled DSLR camera to a RED ONE—an industry workhorse. The Arri Alexa or the high-speed Phantom are capable of capturing over one million frames per second! It's unlikely, however, that those editing Arri or RED footage will use Photoshop because these are professional video cameras that can cost up to six figures fully loaded and are used by experienced videographers who are more likely using Adobe Premiere Pro, Avid Media Composer, or Apple Final Cut Pro for their editing.

But Photoshop is easy to use and allows you to quickly achieve great results. Most likely, your focus (excuse the pun) is on using a point-and-shoot camera or an HDSLR (High-Definition Single Lens Reflex)-capable camera from manufacturers such as Canon, Nikon, or Sony. The principles are the same whichever camera you are using. I'll mostly reference the DSLR cameras that I use, which are currently the Canon 5D Mark II and the Canon 5D Mark III.

The whole HDSLR revolution began a few years ago when Canon announced the Canon 5D Mark II in December 2008. It was then that everything changed. An affordable full-frame camera capable of full high-definition video was finally within everyone's reach. The first amazing aspect of a DSLR camera is the size of its image sensor compared to the tiny image sensor in a current camcorder.

With a larger sensor, the camera is capable of shooting with a narrower depth of field (DOF). This means that you can shoot the subject sharp with the background out of focus, which produces the coveted cinematic effect (**FIGURE 1.1**). This look wasn't possible with video before unless you used a very expensive and heavy camera.

Depth of field describes how much detail can be kept in focus over a certain distance. When both near and far objects are in focus at the same time, this is called a deep focus and the image has a large DOF, very popular for landscape and nature-type shots as it shows maximum detail. If a closer object is sharp and everything behind it appears soft and blurry, this is known as a shallow depth of field and is popular for portrait and interview shots, as it minimizes distracting details. Depth of field is controlled by aperture. If the aperture opening is small (measured in f-stops), say f22 or f32, this produces a large depth of field. If the aperture opening is large, say at f2,8, then you'll have a shallow depth of field.

FIGURE 1.1 Shallow depth of
field (top) versus a large depth
of field (bottom).

Did the people at Canon even realize the revolution they would start with these cameras? Established filmmakers like Shane Hurlbut (*Terminator Salvation*, *Act of Valor*) and TV cinematographers like Rodney Charters (*24*, *Shameless*, *Dallas*) rushed to use these cameras. Why would they if they have access to all the high-end gear? The reason is that the cameras are small, light, and cheap. For example, over 20 5D Mark IIs were used to make a large portion of the film *Act of Valor*, which features real-life, active, U.S. Navy Seals in action. The cameras were strapped onto helmets, mounted on actors, and moved in ways that you can't move a large heavy camera. They were placed under cars, thrown, shot at, dunked in water, and more.

The good news is that you have access to the same equipment used in the making of major motion pictures and episodic television. Yes! Brand-new filmmakers are springing up everywhere. For example, check out the work of Freddie Wong on YouTube. Now, I'm not saying that you have to be an aspiring filmmaker to shoot HDSLR. Event and portrait photographers can add video to their lists of services and products. Even enthusiasts and soccer moms can now enjoy the highest quality of video.

Lenses

Today, you can use a variety of lenses—wide-angle, telephoto, prime, tilt-shift, fisheye, and even fun lenses like Lensbaby (**FIGURE 1.2**)—to shoot video. If you're using a DSLR camera, you can use your existing lens.

FIGURE 1.2 A Lensbaby Composer Pro with a Sweet 35 Optic, mounted on a Canon 5D Mk II.

If you're shopping for cinema lenses, a *prime lens* is a good choice. It has a fixed focal length (it doesn't zoom) and might be a 50mm or an 85mm. The advantage of a prime lens is that is it very sharp because the glass doesn't have to be designed for different focal lengths. Another advantage of prime lenses is they tend to be very fast, meaning that the aperture opening is large and allows in more light. Look for 1.4 or 1.8 as common maximum apertures for prime lenses. These apertures allow you to shoot in low light as well as that coveted narrow depth of field. How do you zoom a prime lens? Well, you actually use your feet. You'll need to change the camera position to frame your shot.

Memory Cards

When you choose memory cards for your camera, make sure that you get the fastest cards available to allow the camera to write to the card and capture all the video. If the card is too slow, the data can't be written fast enough, which causes a recording error. In practice, most modern cards are fast enough.

Also, make sure that you have a card reader and a laptop handy. Cards will fill up quickly while shooting video, so it's a good idea to "dump" the data from one card to a laptop while you are shooting with another card. You can plug the camera into the laptop and transfer data directly, but this will tie up the camera, drain its batteries, and take longer than a cheap card reader.

Dynamic vs. Static Camera Moves

One big mistake new videographers make is moving the camera too much and trying to follow movement everywhere. Sweeping pans and constant movement of the camera can result in you moving viewers' stomachs more so than their emotions. I suggest, at least when you are beginning, that you use a tripod. Frame the shot as you would if you were taking a photograph, and let the movement happen within the frame. When the camera isn't moved during a shot, it is called a *static shot*. Obviously, there will be times when you'll need to move the camera, but avoid doing so as much as possible when you're just beginning to shoot video. When the camera is moving during a shot, it is called a *dynamic shot*.

Static Shots

As mentioned, a static shot is one where the camera is stationary. Leaving the camera stationary allows the viewer to concentrate on the movement that is happening in the frame rather than the camera drawing attention to itself with movements. The majority of your shots should be static. They are stable and the viewer doesn't get motion sickness. Keep the camera on a tripod and frame so that the action can happen without moving the camera to capture it.

Dynamic Camera Moves

When you do decide to move the camera while shooting, you can perform two sets of moves. The first is when the camera doesn't change position. These are the types of moves you can use when the camera is in a stationary tripod:

- **Pan.** The camera rotates on the y-axis. This is the kind of move you use while following action or actors to keep them in the frame.

- **Tilt.** The camera rotates on the x-axis following a vertical position, such as when you scan a skyscraper from bottom to top.

- **Roll.** During a roll, you actually rotate the camera at an angle. This shouldn't be done too often because it can be nauseating.

- **Zoom.** The camera doesn't change position, but you adjust the focal distance of the lens.

The second set of movements is accomplished by actually moving the camera position:

- **Dolly.** The camera's position moves from the left or right. This creates a lot of parallax where the foreground moves faster than the background, and it can build a sense of depth.

- **Boom.** The actual height of the camera is changed. This can be accomplished handheld by crouching and then standing, using a ladder, or more commonly on a larger budget by using a crane.

- **Truck (dolly in and out).** The camera moves closer or farther away from the action. The combination of a dolly in and a dolly out is called a *truck move*. This produces a different look than a zoom because of the relationship of an object to its background.

Stabilization

If you've already shot some video, you'll have discovered that it's very difficult to keep your shots still if you aren't using a tripod. Camera shake is undesirable, and unlike camcorders, not too many cameras have built-in stabilization just yet. Some lenses have image stabilizers built in, and they can work fairly well. But no matter what, you will need a solid shooting platform.

The most common type of stabilization is a tripod. You could use a monopod too if you like, but I've found that in many DSLR shooting situations a monopod does not provide a stable shooting platform. If static shots are all that are required, an existing photography setup will work fine. However, if you plan on performing any camera movement, you'll need to change the ballhead to a fluid head. Fluid heads or video tripods can actually be very inexpensive. They are designed to pan smoothly and work better than a ballhead for video work. A ballhead works great for photography but doesn't have smooth enough movement for video.

If you are moving the camera's position dynamically, many accessories are available. You could use a full-track and dolly but that might be a bit much for many of you. It's surprising what you can do with a skateboard, shopping cart, or even a roller-board bag. A simple rail system can also be used for some subtle camera moves.

In the world of camera-motion accessories, a few other portable assets stand out.

The Aviator Travel Jib

An interesting newcomer to the gear world is the Aviator Travel Jib (**FIGURE 1.3**), which allows for high-production quality at a low price and maximum ease of use. It's a portable crane that fits on a tripod and extends to 6 feet, is made of carbon fiber and weighs just 2¾ pounds (supporting cameras up to 7.5 lbs!), and sets up in under a minute. Use it to shoot weddings, sports, or other productions that require a high-end look, without breaking the bank. You can get the camera up really high for an aerial shot that pans a room or crowd of people.

FIGURE 1.3 The Aviator Travel Jib.

Handheld Stabilizers

You can capture some great handheld shots once you have a little more experience, but you'll need to consider some stabilizing equipment to pull this off well. Tons of gear have been released lately that allow for stable handheld shooting. The main player in DSLR accessories is Red Rock Micro. The company makes a modular system that includes shoulder mounting gear, stabilizers, focus pullers, and more. Steadicam makes a system that allows for a lot of smooth movement (**FIGURE 1.4**). In addition, a slew of companies make cheaper knock-offs and different types of gear that you can use to stabilize your handheld shots.

FIGURE 1.4 The Steadicam Merlin offers great stabilization for a handheld shot on an HDSLR.

Camera Settings

Some basic camera settings will help you shoot better video. In photography, getting the correct exposure is a combination of the amount of light that strikes the image sensor and the amount of time that the sensor is exposed to that light. Settings that control the light are aperture, shutter speed, and ISO:

■ **Aperture** is the size of the opening of the lens. As mentioned previously, the larger the opening, the more light that comes in, which also reduces the depth of field.

■ **Shutter speed**, more accurately called the exposure time in digital cameras, is the amount of time the aperture is open. Fast shutter speeds freeze motion, whereas slower speeds cause motion blur.

■ **ISO** is the sensitivity of the image sensor. Turn it higher and you need less light through the lens to achieve the same exposure, which also produces more image noise.

Typically, a photographer chooses the desired depth of field with the aperture and then adjusts the exposure time (shutter speed) to get the exposure. If the exposure time is too slow, motion blur will occur. The ISO is usually turned to a higher setting to compensate. But the clincher in video is that you can't work this way! Let me explain and offer some guidance.

Motion Blur in Video

If you shoot video using a shutter speed of 1/125 of a second, each frame is very sharp and crisp. The problem with this is that the video looks stuttery due to sharpness of the frames. What is needed is a little bit of natural motion blur. When you slow down the shutter speed, the individual frames look a little blurry. That's OK when you're shooting video because the resulting motion will look very smooth and fluid when the frames play back.

The recommended formula for the shutter speed is 1/double the frame rate. For example, when you're shooting at 30 frames per second (fps), a shutter speed of 1/60 of a second is ideal. At 24 fps, you should shoot at 1/50 of a second (there is no 1/48). This isn't a hard and fast rule, but it's a good guideline to work from if you want the appearance of smooth motion.

Getting Correct Exposure

Using a fixed shutter speed changes the equation for maintaining the correct exposure because you've removed one of the factors used in controlling exposure. For example, take into account shooting with the aperture open for a shallow depth of field effect. How do you control exposure? In addition to changing the light, you have two options.

To get more light into the camera, you can turn up the ISO. Making the sensor more sensitive will allow a correct exposure without adjusting the shutter speed. This is typical for low-light situations.

FIGURE 1.5 A variable neutral density filter by Schneider Optics.

What about the opposite situation when there is too much light? This will happen a lot when you're shooting outdoors. If you close down the aperture, you will reduce the amount of light striking the sensor, but you will also have a larger depth of field, causing you to lose the cinematic effect. The solution is to attach a neutral density (ND) filter to your lens. These filters come in different strengths and are available as variable options that you can adjust. In essence, an ND filter is a tinted piece of glass, like sunglasses for your lens. Some typical types screw onto the end of a lens, such as those made by Tiffen. You can also purchase a matte box and mount it in front of your lens. A matte box makes it easy to quickly pop filters in and out. A variable ND filter (**FIGURE 1.5**) simplifies things because you can actually change the amount of density by rotating a piece of polarized glass over a second piece of polarized glass.

Focus

Some cameras include the ability to auto focus or follow focus during the entire shoot. However, it's a better practice to get a sharp focus on the subject before rolling and then use manual focus. The reason for this is to prevent the camera's focus from wandering. I'm sure you have experienced this problem. The focus sometimes drifts as the camera is searching for the perfect focus. The best way to keep focus is to manually change the focus as the subject or camera moves. In fact, you can purchase a follow focus adjustment from companies such as Red Rock Micro. This attachment is geared so that your adjustments are more sensitive and thus more accurate. Companies like Zacuto also make attachments called screen magnifiers that fasten over the screen of the camera backs and allow you to see an enlarged view. This allows the operator to see the subject better and achieve a tack-sharp focus at all times.

Lighting Basics

An essential part of video is lighting. To capture visual elements, you need light. Basically, there are two types of light: natural, sometimes called available light, and artificial (lighting equipment). You should also be aware of the three properties of light: quantity, quality, and direction.

Light Quantity

The quantity of light is the easiest to describe. How light or dark is it? How much light is there? To get a clean image, there must be sufficient light. Outdoors, during the day, there is usually plenty of sunlight, even on a cloudy day. Indoors is another matter entirely. If large windows are facing the sun, there could possibly be enough natural light to get a decent exposure. But when light is insufficient, you need to add light. You can add light by introducing additional light sources, such as supplementary lights like overhead office lights, or professional lighting equipment. Additional light sources can also include light reflectors, such as mirrors, reflector panels, bounce cards, and the like. All of these light sources are discussed later in the "Lighting Equipment" section.

The simple presence of light will not make a good shot on camera unless there is enough of it. For a lit subject to actually look good, you also need to address the next property of light, which is quality.

Light Quality

The quality of light boils down to the amount of contrast in the light. If high-contrast, sharp, dark, hard-edged shadows are present and the highlights are stark, the light is called *hard light*. On the other hand, if the shadows have soft edges and the highlights are feathered and even, the light is called *soft light*.

The quality of the light is determined mainly by the relative size of the light source in relation to the object being illuminated. A good example is the outdoors. In the middle of the day when the sun is at its highest point, the light is hard and unappealing. Why is this? Isn't the sun a massive source of light and many times the size of the earth? Well, yes, but recall that I used the phrase "relative size" of the light source. Because the sun is so far away from the earth, it's actually a very small and focused light source. However, on an overcast day, the sunlight becomes a very soft and diffused light, which is very appealing. The reason this occurs is because the cloud cover scatters or "diffuses" the light source. When light is diffused, it travels in many different directions, which softens the appearance of shadows. The resulting effect is that the entire sky becomes a giant light source.

The example of an overcast sky proves that you can change the quantity of light. And you can do this by changing the size of the light source in two possible ways: by moving the light closer to the subject or by using light modifiers.

A light modifier alters the size of a light source. Common examples of modifiers are umbrellas, diffusion fabrics that you shoot through, and either panels or softboxes. You can also bounce the light off different surfaces, white walls, and even foam core panels to enlarge the source of light relative to the subject (see the section "Light Modifiers").

Light Direction

The third property of light is its direction. What angle is the light coming from? When light strikes a subject, it not only illuminates the subject, but also casts shadows on the opposite side of the light. The angle of illumination affects the shadow. Have you ever noticed later in the day that shadows tend to grow and stretch, whereas in the middle of the day with light overhead the shadows are very small and short? What can you learn from this? The more acute the angle of the light, the more shadow it will cast. If you want to show the texture of a subject, use a hard light that is at a steep angle and skimmed across the surface of the subject. If you want to disguise texture, such as wrinkles on a face, using a soft light shone directly at the subject will minimize the appearance of shadow. Changing the direction of the light will actually shape the object.

Shape

You can make an object look very flat by placing a large light source directly in front of it. If you want to show more shape, make sure the light strikes the subject from an angle. Although this type of angled light can add dimension to the subject, it will also cast a shadow on the opposite side, which you can minimize by introducing an additional light source. The additional light source is commonly known as *fill light*. Fill light shouldn't be as powerful as the main light source; instead, it should be directed into the shadow area to illuminate or fill in the shadows. The use of a silver or white reflector on the opposite side of the main light can be enough to fill in the light. Other times additional lights can be used as fill light. This is known as *two-point lighting*. It's common to use more than one reflector to fill in shadows. Typically, most photographers and videographers use a small reflector under the chin of a person to soften the shadows on the face and neck.

Separation

When a subject is illuminated, sometimes it can blend into the background and look flat. When you need the subject to pop or stand out from the background, you must create a separation light. Separation light illuminates the edges of the subject from behind (rim lighting). This light is known by several names: *back light*, *hair-light* (if it's high and behind a person), and *kicker*—the most common name for this separation light in the video world because it "kicks" the subject off the background.

Lighting Configurations

The most common type of video lighting used indoors is three-point lighting. The setup includes a main light, a fill light, and a back light. See the illustration of three-point lighting in **FIGURE 1.6** and **FIGURE 1.7**. Figure 1.6 shows three light sources used, and Figure 1.7 shows two lights and a reflector.

FIGURE 1.6 Three-point lighting using three lights.

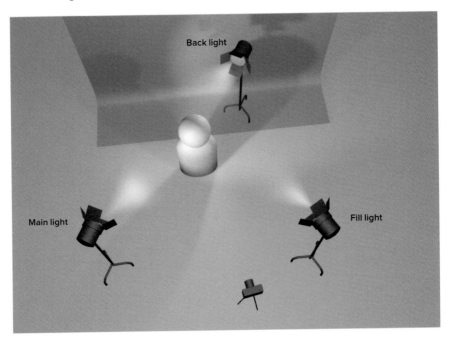

FIGURE 1.7 Three-point lighting using two lights and a reflector.

Outdoor Lighting

As mentioned earlier, one of the challenges of shooting outdoors is controlling sunlight. On an overcast day, it's very easy, but on a bright sunny day, what can you do? You could shoot your subject in shade. Alternatively (and very common), you can use a diffusion panel. The panel is placed between the sun and the subject to soften the shadows. The diffusion in itself will make a huge difference. But a reflector is usually also used to bounce some fill light into the shadows on the opposite side of the sun.

Light Color

Light isn't transparent. All light has a color, and several factors affect the light's color:

- **Heat.** When you look at fire, on the outside of a flame you'll notice that the color is red. Red is the coolest part of the flame, whereas white is the hottest part. If you were to heat up that flame by concentrating it with a blow torch, the color will be blue.

- **Chemical makeup.** Chemical makeup applies to artificial light. The actual process of creating the light will vary the color. Incandescent light, the common light bulb, is a yellowish color. Fluorescent light is more of a green or blue color. Recently, however, both of these light sources are moving more toward a white light.

- **Natural light.** Moonlight is blue. As the sun rises and starts to set, its light is scattered by particulates in the atmosphere, filtered through dust and smog, and becomes a warmer, more golden color.

Light color is known as *color temperature* and is measured on a scale known as the Kelvin scale. Daylight balanced light is 5600K.

Setting White Balance

When you are shooting video, it's important to set the correct white balance setting on your camera so the color of the video looks correct to the viewer. A color cast (footage has an unwanted colored tint) can be fixed in Photoshop, but you'll achieve vastly superior results by shooting with the correct settings in the first place.

You need to change the white balance settings on your camera to match the scene's light: sunlight, cloudy day, fluorescent, incandescent, and so on. The best option is to use a custom white balance if your camera supports this feature. To obtain a custom white balance, place either a white card or a clean sheet of white paper in the location that you will be shooting. Zoom into the white source until it fills the frame and take a photograph (press the white balance button on a camcorder). Choose "custom white balance" on your camera and select the photograph of the white frame as the custom white balance. The colors will be balanced. Redo this process if you change any of the lighting or location.

Lighting Equipment

The equipment you'll need for shooting video should consist of constant light sources. Strobes and flashes will not work for shooting video because they are not continuous sources of light. Let's explore some of the main types of lights available for video.

Video Light Types

There are several different types of constant lights available for shooting video. The choices will depend on the look you are going for and the budget.

- **Hot lights.** These lights use a filament bulb to create illumination and are known as hot lights because they can get very toasty when left on for any amount of time. The different types of filaments in the vacuum bulbs produce light of varying strengths. The power of these lights are measured in watts. Hot lights can vary from a simple bedside lamp to expensive, high-powered Arri lights used in movie production.

- **Fluorescents.** Fluorescent light is created by running an electric charge through mercury vapor, which illuminates phosphor. These lights are also called cool lights because they don't produce much heat. I prefer to use fluorescents for video production because they are cool to the touch, low in power consumption, and daylight balanced (5600K). They are also lightweight, making them more portable than hot lights. The clear market leader in fluorescent light banks used in video production is Kino Flo (**FIGURE 1.8**) because they maintain a consistent color temperature, they are flicker free, and they have a dimmable ballast.

TIP The advantage of LEDs are that they're very bright (avoid looking directly into an undiffused LED), thin, lightweight, and have very low power consumption. LEDs are ideal for taking on location.

- **LEDs.** A technology that is constantly improving is LED lights (light-emitting diodes). LEDs used to be used solely as indicators in electronic equipment and even made their way into digital watches in the 1980s. Recent advances in technology have enabled LEDs to become very powerful and emit a lot of light. Many cars now use LED lights as running lights and taillights. These lights have found their way into photographic and video lights as well. The most prominent brand is Litepanels (**FIGURE 1.9**), which has been taking over TV studios for several years now.

FIGURE 1.8 My preferred setup using Kino Flo Diva Light 400s. Crystal is kind enough to sit in as a model.

FIGURE 1.9
Litepanel LED lights.

Light Modifiers

Regardless of the actual light type you use, you can use several tools to modify or control the light. These modifiers fall into the families of diffuse (soften), directors (angle and spread), and bounce (reflect). Some of the most common types of equipment include the following:

TIP This book is not intended as a complete course on lighting. For more detailed lighting instruction, check out www.software-cinema.com and learn from the greats, such as the late Dean Collins.

- **Diffusers.** Diffusers soften the light by creating a larger light source than the naked light. Softboxes and panels fall into this category. A panel can be as simple as a bed sheet and as complex as a frame with light-transmitting material stretched across it. This material is placed between the source of illumination and the subject. A diffuser allows light to pass through it but scatters the light and spreads it across its surface. This softens the light source and can be used in direct sunlight or in the studio whenever a light is too harsh for the intended shoot.

  A softbox is a reflecting box of light with a removable diffuser that affixes to the front of a light (**FIGURE 1.10**), which increases the size of the light and produces an even and soft light. The larger the softbox, the softer the light.

- **Flags.** A flag (or French flag) is a dark, nonreflecting piece of material (shown in **FIGURE 1.11**) that is placed between the light source and the subject or camera to block light. It can be a store-bought flag, or it can just be a piece of black painted cardboard or foam core. When placed between the light source and the subject, it controls where light strikes the subject. When placed between the light source and the camera, it's used to prevent lens flare (which occurs when the direct light bounces off the glass of the lens).

- **Barn doors.** Barn doors are synonymous with so-called Hollywood lights. They are rectangles on hinges mounted on the edge of lights. You can use barn doors to control where the light falls. The doors can be closed to create a small area of illumination or opened to allow the light to spill freely. They are useful because you can adjust each door individually to provide maximum control.

- **Grids.** A grid or soft eggcrate is placed over a light source to focus the light spill. When a grid is placed over a light, the width of the beam is narrowed, which illuminates a smaller area. You should use grids when you want to create a spotlight effect and minimize light spill.

- **Bounce.** Bounce light is used to reflect the available light or an added light source. Most commonly, bounce light is used as fill light to fill in shadows. These lights can range from handheld panels made of a white, silver, or gold material to mirrors or panels. The reflecting panels can be as simple as white foam core material or even sheets of paper. Bounce cards are typically placed on the opposite side of the light source and reflect the light back into the shadow areas of the subject. Reflectors can be held in place by using stands (Figure 1.11), asking an assistant to help, or even having the subject hold one or more.

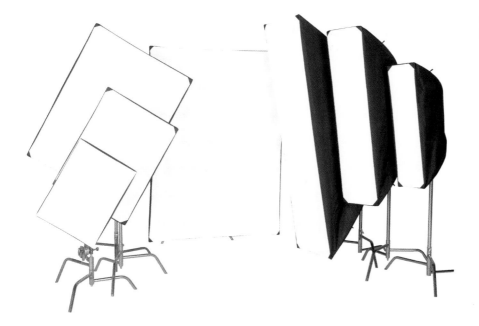

FIGURE 1.10 Chimera lightbanks (softboxes).

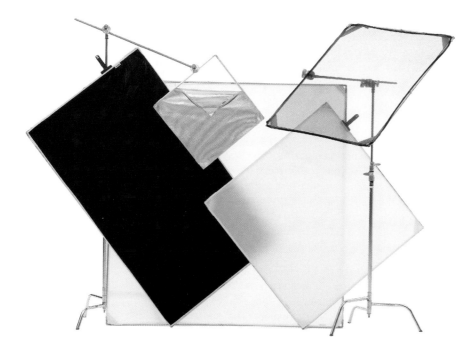

FIGURE 1.11 A collection of Chimera panels, including diffusion, bounce, and flag.

Capturing good audio is also important for great video content. This is especially true if you are recording an interview. For the best quality, external microphones are commonly used, as the quality of the in-build microphones in cameras are usually less than great (just look at the tiny pinhole in the front of a DSLR camera, for example).

Whichever way you use to get audio into your camera, beware of the auto recording levels, or Auto Gain Control (AGC), setting. Make sure you turn off this setting and set the recording levels manually. If you turn on AGC, you will likely get a very noisy signal followed by a sudden surge of noise as it tries to find the volume and level it out. Then, in long moments of silence, it will boost the ambient (background) noise. The result of AGC is very undesirable!

To learn more about audio, check out Chapter 5, "Bringing Video Alive with Sound," which is devoted entirely to this essential subject.

Computer Requirements

The preceding crash course on video production is intended to get you up to speed quickly. But because this book is about the process of editing video, let's talk computer hardware for a second. I'll assume that your computer meets the minimum specifications to run Photoshop CS6, so I'll discuss some details that will make a difference in computer performance during editing. It doesn't matter if you are using a Mac or a Windows computer; the principles are the same. Photoshop functions the same on both platforms and has the same feature set. The only difference is the modifier keys: The Mac uses Command/Option/Control/Delete; Windows uses Ctrl/Alt/right-click/Backspace.

GPU

As you probably know, a GPU is a graphics processing unit. Every computer has a video card that powers the graphics that you see onscreen. Advances in the video card now include an onboard GPU that handles the graphics on this piece of hardware. A GPU handles much more than just displaying an image on the screen. These video cards actually accelerate a lot of the visual rendering, taking this load off the main CPU. A combination of 64-bit, GPU acceleration and software optimization is called the Mercury Playback Engine by Adobe. Mercury means that you will experience high performance when you're working with video.

The bottom line is that a good video card is becoming just as necessary as lots of RAM or a fast computer. If you are buying a new computer, avoid integrated graphics and make sure you get a machine with a dedicated GPU. You can also upgrade the video card on older computers. NVIDIA makes a line of affordable cards under the GeForce moniker. If you have extra cash and desire the ultimate in performance, consider shelling out top dollar for the Quadro FX line of cards (FIGURE 1.12). As a bonus, these cards work wonders with 3D too.

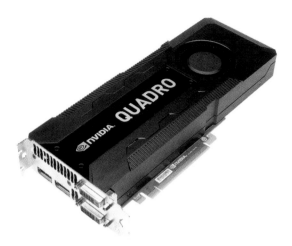

FIGURE 1.12
NVIDIA Quadro GPU.

RAM

Many years ago it was said that you can never have too much RAM. This remains true today as well, especially with video. When you are previewing your video in Photoshop, it uses what's known as *RAM preview,* which means that the RAM holds the data for you to watch. The more RAM you have, the longer the clips you can view in real time. Not only is RAM previewing RAM intensive, but any process in Photoshop is as well. RAM is faster than accessing the hard drive. Although you can run Photoshop on 4 GB of RAM, I recommend at least 8 GB, and at the time of this writing, you will be even happier with 16 GB.

External Drives/Scratch Disks

Photoshop supports multiple scratch drives. When it's working, Photoshop writes a file that can be up to ten times the size of the working file. This information is written to RAM, and once the RAM fills up, the files are then written to a scratch disk. The scratch disk performs the task of RAM but is slower. Some people install a dedicated scratch disk and use it only for working in Photoshop. The advantage is that the drive doesn't fragment or slow down because there is nothing else on it.

Solid-State Drive (SSD)

The solid-state drive has no moving parts and relies on Flash storage. The main result of this is speed. A mechanical arm on a regular drive has to move in order to access the drive; a solid state doesn't, so this can result in up to ten times faster performance. Not only can an SDD write faster, but it also starts up and accesses data much faster. For best performance, use an SSD as a startup drive and also use it as a scratch drive to speed up Photoshop's operations.

Now that you have all the background you need for shooting and equipment, you can start to capture all your footage. Happy shooting! From here on, you'll focus on what to do with all the video that you've shot. Without any more ramblings from me, let's get started!

CHAPTER 2

ORGANIZING ASSETS IN ADOBE LIGHTROOM AND ADOBE BRIDGE

IT'S SO EXCITING AND EASY TO SHOOT VIDEO THESE DAYS. In the excitement, we forget how quickly we can accumulate a large library of footage. Imagine a physical library, where all the books are stacked up in piles. In this manner, it would be very difficult to find anything and the library would lose its usefulness. Similarly, it's important that you organize and manage your digital assets (your footage and photographs). Proper digital asset management ensures that you can quickly find something when you need it, which makes all the difference to a busy professional.

Adobe Bridge and Adobe Lightroom make it very easy to organize and locate footage and photographs. In this chapter, we will look at some of their features and how you can organize your digital life.

Digital Asset Management

Video used to be shot on magnetic tape, which was then digitized through a process commonly known as *capturing*. The workflow consisted of attaching a video device to a computer with the tape inserted and choosing, for example, a Log and Capture feature in the editing software. The video would then play all the way through while the editing software digitized it and stored it onto a disk drive. Some of the more savvy shooters captured live to a computer with a capture card and the use of software such as Adobe On Location. When tapeless cameras were introduced, shooting onto solid-state Flash drives became the norm because it was much more efficient.

So once you have a Flash drive full of video, what do you do with it? How do you store and access it for editing? This chapter will help you prepare your video and assets for editing in Adobe Photoshop.

Whatever media you are shooting to, whether it is Compact Flash, Micro SD, or a mobile device, you need to transfer your footage to a working drive. You can choose to use a hard drive on your computer or an external drive. The advantage of using an internal drive is speed. But an external drive allows the project to be portable; you can move from computer to computer and your project and all the assets are always with you.

It doesn't really matter where you save your files. The important factor is to make sure you have a system that allows you to find and access your files when you need them. As a professional, I am very careful and consistent with the way I store my files, using both folder-based and metadata organizational methods.

TIP Assets are any form of video, audio, or images and they can be used in assembling a project. Digital assets are digital files. Digital asset management (DAM) is the art of storing and organizing digital files in a way that you can easily find them when needed.

Folder-based Management Systems

Folder-based management systems are a bit old school but are still valid. Media is stored in a way that is easy to find and navigate. For example, you can create a folder called Video, and then save all your video files in this folder. You can then categorize the files further by creating subfolders with names like Studio, Models, Locations, and other appropriate names. If you want to drill down even more, you can create subfolders within a subfolder with the names of the individual models or actual places under Locations. Some people sort files even further and organize them by individual shoot or date.

The important aspect of a folder-based system is consistency in the naming and filing of these folders. They become much like a digital filing cabinet that allows you to easily retrieve the images and footage when you need them.

Metadata-based Management Systems

A more modern way of organizing digital assets is with the metadata-based organizational method. Metadata is data about data. This data is attached to the digital files in the form of XMP. Basically XMP is an XML text file that contains information about the asset and includes the type of camera used, lens, shooting time, and other capture data. You can also add additional information, such as keywords and descriptions. All this information is accessed and edited through Adobe Bridge and Lightroom.

Using tools such as keywords allows you to search and find assets across multiple folders and drives. This is faster and more efficient than using just folders.

Say, for example, you have a picture of a model at the beach. Would you file it under beach or model? What if the model is holding a designer bag and you also want to organize by brands of bags? You would need to create three copies of the image and place each image in a separate folder. But what if you retouch one image? How do you know which one is retouched? This is where metadata rules. You can simply attach three keywords to the single image and it will appear in all of the searches.

As mentioned earlier, I use a hybrid of both systems by copying all my assets to drives and putting them safely into folders sorted by shoot and main topic. Then I add metadata immediately while the files are still manageable. I add keywords as soon as possible so that I can easily find images and video at a later date. We'll look at adding and filtering searches by keywords in Lightroom in the "Metadata for Sorting and Organizing" section later in the chapter.

Two Adobe applications, Adobe Bridge and Adobe Lightroom, are ideal to help you add metadata tagging, search for files, and view those files. This chapter isn't designed as a full walk-through of these applications, but you will learn the basics that you need to organize your media.

Using Adobe Bridge with Video

TIP To load a folder, drag it to the preview window and the directory path will change to the folder you dragged. All the contents will display in the window.

Adobe Bridge is an asset management application that is part of the Adobe Creative Suite or Adobe Creative Cloud, or bundled with Photoshop if you purchased a stand-alone version. It works really well to organize your photos and your videos too.

To transfer your video to your computer, it's best if you attach a card reader to your computer. Using a card reader for transfer is faster than using your camera, plus it doesn't drain the camera's batteries. Copy all your media to the hard drive or external drive from where you will be working, and then follow these steps:

1. Launch Adobe Bridge (**FIGURE 2.1**).

2. Click the Folders tab and a directory tree appears. Click the folders to navigate to the same folder where you copied your assets. You can navigate to this book's **footage** folder if you want to see those videos as thumbnails here. Thumbnails will display in the content window. Footage will display as a thumbnail just like an image does.

TIP You can enlarge the size of any window by dragging the edges of the panes. Increase the size of thumbnails by dragging the lever at the bottom of the main Adobe Bridge window.

3. To view the video in the preview window, click its thumbnail. Click the arrow button to play the video and watch it. You will also hear audio during playback.

FIGURE 2.1 The Adobe Bridge main window.

A Navigation
B Footage thumbnails
C Preview window
D Metadata

Folder Cruising

Folder Cruising is a neat feature in Adobe Bridge. Directly above the Folders panel you'll see that the directory structure displays a path known as breadcrumbs (**FIGURE 2.2**). Right-click on any of the arrows to display all the subfolders under that portion of the path. Select a subfolder to navigate there. Alternatively, if you choose the option Show Items from Subfolders (**FIGURE 2.3**), you'll see all images and footage from all the subfolders as well as the current folder.

TIP In your downloads you'll find a Photoshop-CAFE training video called **bridge_keywords.mp4**. It walks you through working with Adobe Bridge and keywording.

FIGURE 2.2 Bread crumb navigation.

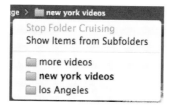

FIGURE 2.3 Options to view subfolders.

Favorites

As you may have discovered, it can take a little effort to navigate to certain folders. The good news is that you can easily save all the folder locations as Favorites.

1. Navigate to the desired folder and select it (**FIGURE 2.4**). Try any one of the lesson folders in your downloaded files if you'd like.

2. Either drag the folder to the Favorites tab or simply right-click the folder to reveal a context menu. Choose the Add to Favorites option (**FIGURE 2.5**).

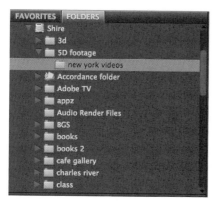

FIGURE 2.4 The Folders panel with a folder selected.

FIGURE 2.5 The context menu.

3. Click the Favorites tab and you'll notice that your folder is now listed. Click the name of the folder to open it in Adobe Bridge (FIGURE 2.6). All your Favorites will be saved even when you close Adobe Bridge. It might be a good idea to spend a few moments organizing your folders and Favorites before proceeding. Investing the time now will pay off in the long run.

FIGURE 2.6 The Favorites panel showing its contents.

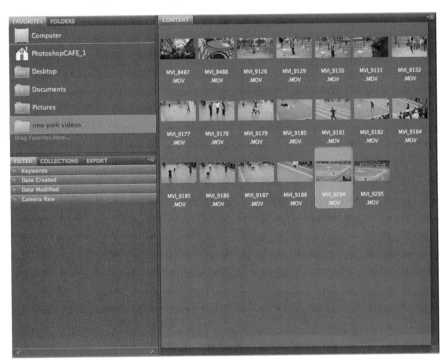

Getting Footage into Lightroom

Lightroom is a lot like Adobe Bridge in that it can manage assets and metadata. Where Lightroom differs is that it's more robust and has many more features and capabilities. Lightroom was originally designed just for managing photos, but version 3 introduced the ability to manage video footage. Even more features are available in Lightroom 4, which I'll discuss in this chapter. Lightroom is designed as a catalog that can manage large numbers of images and video, and its performance is noticeably faster and smoother than Adobe Bridge.

This section does not contain an exhaustive overview of Lightroom. For more information on Lightroom, feel free to access my 10-hour video at photoshopCAFE.com/lightroom if you need it. Here I'll just brief you on the very basics you need to work with video and integrate your workflow with Photoshop. I'll assume that if you are reading this section, you are already using Lightroom to some degree.

I take a slightly different approach to importing assets. Rather than moving files to a location and then referencing them (you can still do that if you desire), you can actually use Lightroom to import the images.

Importing Footage from a Card Reader

For very little money, you can get a card reader that will simplify the task of loading the content into your computer from the camera's card.

1. Insert the card reader into your computer and launch Lightroom.

2. Click the Import button at the lower left of the screen (**FIGURE 2.7**).

   The Import dialog appears (**FIGURE 2.8**).

FIGURE 2.7 The main Lightroom window and the Import button.

FIGURE 2.8 The Import dialog minimized.

3. Click the maximize button if the Import dialog is minimized to display all the options.

4. When you use a card reader, Lightroom usually displays it at the top left. Otherwise, navigate to the source with the footage on it (Camera Card).

5. Click the Copy option at the top center of the screen. This will ensure that a copy of the assets is placed in the desired location. The Move option will also work, but because it will delete the originals from the card, it's best to use the Copy option and then erase the files from the card when you're certain that everything transferred over safely.

CAUTION! If you use the Add option, the footage files will be added to the Lightroom catalog only without actually moving any files. This means that as soon as you remove the card reader, the footage will be offline and lost when the card is formatted.

6. Choose a home for your footage by clicking the To field and selecting either an internal or working external drive (**FIGURE 2.9**). If you desire, you can place the footage into a subfolder for better organization.

FIGURE 2.9 The Import dialog is displayed maximized with all the settings in place.

7. Add some keywords and do a little housekeeping at this point as I usually do to make it easier to find the footage at a later date and organize it further. You can add keywords after the fact just as easily. But I make a habit of adding keywords on import because it doesn't take that much time or effort at this stage of the game. Adding keywords to 30,000 images later can become a major task for the procrastinator. We'll discuss keywords in more depth later in the "Metadata for Sorting and Organizing" section.

Adding Footage from a Hard Drive

Chances are that you already have some footage on your hard drive, and you want to manage it with Lightroom. If so, the process isn't that different than importing from a card, but with a couple of minor differences. Use the footage that comes with this book (found in the **footage** folder) if you'd like.

FIGURE 2.10 Select a drive from the Source panel.

1. Launch Lightroom and click the Import button just as you did in the previous example.

2. Navigate to the drive where the footage is stored. All the attached drives will display on the left side of the screen. **FIGURE 2.10** shows that I have six drives attached.

3. Choose the folder that you want to import from and select (add a check mark next to) all the footage that you want to add to the catalog (**FIGURE 2.11**). Notice that video files have a little video badge on them (**FIGURE 2.12**).

FIGURE 2.11 Select files you want to add.

FIGURE 2.12 A video badge indicates this file contains a video clip.

TIP If you need to change the location of any assets, do it from within Lightroom. If you do it outside of Lightroom, the association will be broken. If you move the assets within Lightroom, their physical locations will also change to reflect the move.

4. This time you choose the Add option. Notice that the destination is shown as the Catalog and no destination path is offered. The reason is that you are not moving any files; you are maintaining their original locations and adding them to Lightroom's catalog, allowing Lightroom to manage the files and their metadata. (You can also choose the Copy option and make a copy of the files just like you would if you were importing from a card but you may not want to have two copies of all your footage on your hard drive.)

5. Click the import button to complete import.

Sorting into Collections

Collections are a way that you can sort images and video footage into virtual folders. The folders don't really exist and no assets are moved.

Once you have imported everything into Lightroom, Previous Import is highlighted and the thumbnails are displayed (**FIGURE 2.13**). This is your best opportunity to sort the contents of the import because it's the only time they will be displayed by themselves as a group.

FIGURE 2.13 A completed import.

1. Click on any of the thumbnails and press Command+A (Ctrl+A) to select all of the files.

2. Find Collections on the left pane, click the plus button, and choose Create Collection (**FIGURE 2.14**).

3. Type in the desired name for the collection. Click Inside a Collection Set if you want to nest the collection (**FIGURE 2.15**); otherwise, use the default Top Level option. Make sure the option "Include selected photos" is selected. Don't be fooled by the term *photos;* this terminology also includes video.

FIGURE 2.14 The Create Collection option is listed with other Collections options.

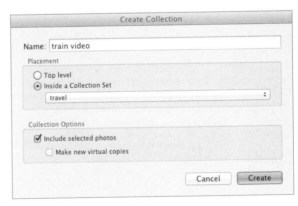

FIGURE 2.15 Creating a collection.

4. Click Create. Your footage is now organized into a collection, and you can access it at any time by clicking its name in the Collections panel (**FIGURE 2.16**).

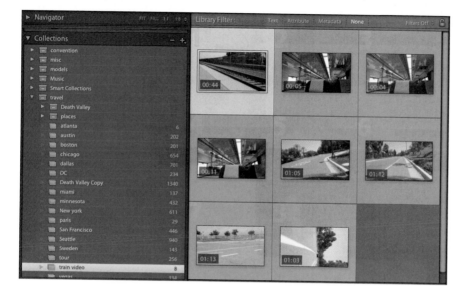

FIGURE 2.16 Viewing a collection.

Metadata for Sorting and Organization

As mentioned earlier, metadata is the best way to tag and locate assets in Lightroom. The single most useful type of metadata is keywords. By adding keyword descriptions, you can make it very easy to search across a category or multiple categories to locate footage.

Adding Keywords

To add keywords, select either an individual thumbnail or multiple thumbnails.

In the Library module, choose the Keywording panel. Enter keywords that best describe the footage, separated by commas (**FIGURE 2.17**). If the keywords have been used before, an auto complete word will appear, thus saving you some typing. It's a good idea to use the auto complete word, because it's best if the keywords you use to describe the same thing are consistent. As a result, searching will be easier later.

FIGURE 2.17 Adding keywords.

Filtering by Keyword

After the keywords are added, it's very easy to locate footage based on the keywords, or many other attributes, by using the Filter bar (FIGURE 2.18). The Filter bar is located at the top of the thumbnails in the Library module. If the Filter bar isn't displayed, you can toggle it on and off by pressing the Backslash (\) key on the keyboard.

FIGURE 2.18 The Filter bar in Lightroom.

To search for keywords in Lightroom, do the following:

1. In the left panel choose a catalog or collection to search through. Selecting All Photographs from the Catalog window will search the entire catalog of images and footage (FIGURE 2.19).

FIGURE 2.19 Setting the scope of the search for the entire catalog.

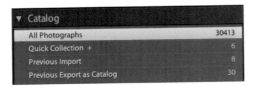

2. Open the Filter bar if it isn't already visible. Click Text to choose text as the filtering criteria.

3. Choose Keywords from the first drop-down list and enter a keyword or multiple keywords.

    The thumbnails will automatically display only the images and footage that meet the search criteria you entered. Be aware that you can combine different search criteria.

4. Experiment with your searches to see what kind of searches you can do and what works best for your workflow (**FIGURE 2.20**).

TIP If you want to save the search results, you can select all and create a new collection from the results. The process is the same as described earlier.

FIGURE 2.20 The results of a keyword search.

You can find all the video footage in a catalog in a snap! Click on the option All Photographs in the Catalog panel. Click Attribute as the search criteria (**FIGURE 2.21**), and then click the video button in the Kind field at the far right (**FIGURE 2.22**). All other assets will be hidden except for the video files.

FIGURE 2.21 Search for video only by first clicking Attribute in the Filter bar.

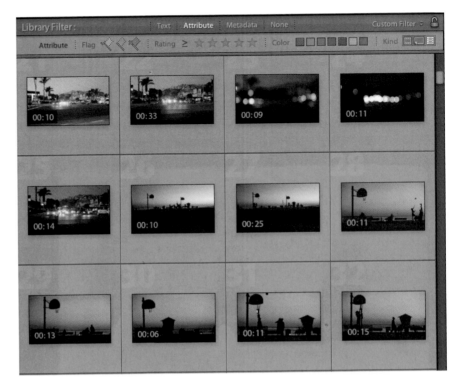

FIGURE 2.22 The video button in the Attributes selector.

Editing Video in Lightroom

Now that you have discovered how to import footage and manage it in Lightroom, let's look at the special features in Lightroom that pertain to video. Although Lightroom does not have a ton of features, those that are available are very useful. You can do a lot in Photoshop (the rest of this book is dedicated to editing in Photoshop), but in Lightroom you can also organize, view, and trim video clips. Not only that but you add some color and tone adjustments. Let's look at each of these functions now.

Viewing Video

Lightroom 3 provided users with the ability to view video, but it was very basic, and you had to launch QuickTime to actually see the video play back. Starting in Lightroom 4 you can now view video directly within the application.

TIP Scrubbing is when you manually drag the playhead through the Timeline to force video playback. It's a quick and easy way to find something in a clip without having to wait or worry about playback speeds. You can scrub forward or backward.

1. Choose a video clip from the thumbnails. Again, you can use a clip from the **footage** folder that is in your downloads here. Double-click to view the clip at a larger size.

2. Click the Play button to watch the video and hear the sound (**FIGURE 2.23**).

3. You can also click and drag the playhead forward and backward to *scrub* through the video.

FIGURE 2.23 Viewing video in Lightroom.

Trimming Video

More advanced controls are hidden in the Timeline, and you can reveal them by clicking the little gear icon ⚙. The Timeline expands to show more options, including a frame preview. You can view and scrub the video here, and even move forward or back a frame at a time by clicking the Rewind and Fast Forward buttons. You can also trim the video clip by setting the In and Out points.

1. To set the In point, click and drag on the left side of the Timeline (FIGURE 2.24). Notice that this sets the beginning point of the clip. The playhead will begin playing from here.

2. To set the Out point of the video, drag from the right side of the Timeline. If you place the playhead on the portion of the video you want to trim, the Out point will snap to the playhead as you drag (FIGURE 2.25). This ensures that you trim exactly where you like.

TIP Setting the In and Out points of a clip is nondestructive. You can change the points at any time. In points and Out points are technical terms for nondestructive trimming. Video will play from the In point and will stop at the Out point. Even though there is more footage in the original clip, it is hidden or excluded from playback by the editing software. The unused beginning is called the head and the unused end is called the tail of the video clip.

FIGURE 2.24 Setting the In point of the video.

FIGURE 2.25 Setting the Out point of the video.

Adding a Look to Video

As stated earlier, you can make adjustments to the look of your video in Lightroom. However, when you choose a video clip and open the Develop module, this rather disappointing message displays: "Video is not supported in Develop" (**FIGURE 2.26**). So what do you do? It's quite simple really; you just need to know a sneaky workaround.

FIGURE 2.26 A frustrating message displays when you try to work with video in the Develop module.

What you need to do is capture a frame of video as an image and make the adjustments to that frame. Fortunately, the engineers at Adobe thought of this solution.

1. In Lightroom, open the file **office.mp4** from the **Ch02** folder of files you downloaded for this book (see the Introduction). Scrub through the clip until you find a frame of the video that best represents the footage that you want to adjust.

2. Make sure the Timeline is in expanded view by clicking the gear icon. In the Timeline panel click the little rectangle next to the gear and choose Capture Frame. An image is created and stacked with the video clip (**FIGURE 2.27**).

3. Choose the image and launch the Develop module (**FIGURE 2.28**).

FIGURE 2.27 Capturing a frame of video.

FIGURE 2.28 The image in the Develop module.

4. Make some adjustments to the image as desired, by moving the adjustment sliders. In this case I created a basic video look by changing some basic Tone settings and adding a little Split Tone (**FIGURES 2.29** and **2.30**). (You can find the preset for these changes in the **video-splittone.lrtemplate** file in the **Ch02** folder.)

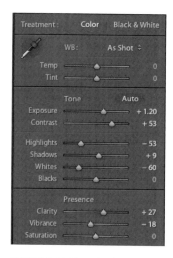

FIGURE 2.29 Some basic adjustments to the captured frame image.

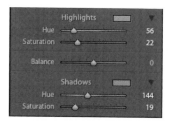

FIGURE 2.30 Some Split Tone adjustments made to the video.

After the look has been created on the image, it's just a matter of transferring it to the video footage (**FIGURE 2.31**).

FIGURE 2.31 The final adjusted image.

5. Click the Presets panel, and then click the plus button to the right of the name Presets. Select all the attributes in the resulting dialog (**FIGURE 2.32**).

FIGURE 2.32
Creating the preset.

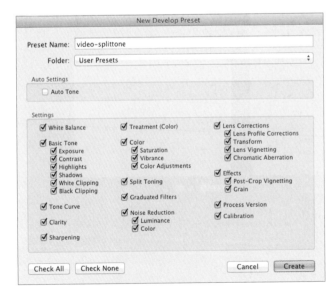

6. Name the preset. In this case, I called it **video-splittone**. (This preset is also provided in the files that accompany the book.) Click Create to make the preset. It will then be listed at the end of the presets under User Presets.

7. Return to the Library module. Select the video, right-click, and choose Develop Settings > User Presets > video-splittone (**FIGURE 2.33**). Click OK to apply the effect.

FIGURE 2.33 Applying a preset to the video clip.

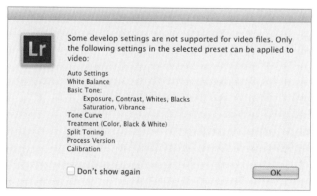

FIGURE 2.34 A list of all the supported Develop Settings appears when you apply a preset to a video clip.

TIP Currently in Lightroom there are several settings not supported for video. **FIGURE 2.34** shows a list of the supported settings.

Notice that the video clip has a cinematic look to it (**FIGURE 2.35**). It's amazing that Lightroom can do this, as it was originally designed as a photograph-only tool. But before you can use these clips, you'll need to export them from Lightroom. You can then bring them into Photoshop for editing, post them up on YouTube, and so on.

Exporting Video

After you've trimmed and colorized your footage, you need to export it from Lightroom and move it to a place where you can use it as footage.

1. In Lightroom, choose the clip you want to export, and then choose File > Export.

    An Export dialog with tons of options appears (**FIGURE 2.36**). Some of these options will be grayed out because you are working with video footage.

2. In this case, save the edited video file to your desktop. Here are the main settings that you can experiment with when you're exporting video from Lightroom:

    ■ Set the export location.

    ■ Choose File Naming if you want to change the name of the file.

    ■ Choose the desired options in the Video section:

      Choose H.264 for the Video Format if you want to export the result of the edited video clip.

      Original will just make a copy of the original unedited clip.

      Set the Quality; Maximum is the best quality but also produces the largest file size. If you want to email the file, consider choosing a lower setting.

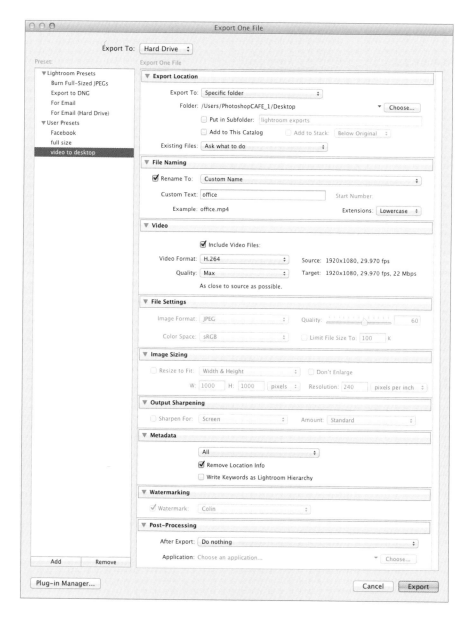

FIGURE 2.36 The Export options.

3. Click the Export button, and the video will be exported to the set location and be ready for your use.

You might want to apply some colorizing effects in Lightroom before moving the video clips into Photoshop. It's not a bad idea, but you should first see what you can do in Photoshop and then make a more informed decision about what you will do in Lightroom and what you will do in Photoshop. Just be aware that you cannot put multiple clips together or add custom sounds and graphics in Lightroom. Read on to learn about all the wonderful things you can do with video in Photoshop.

CHAPTER 3

BASIC EDITING IN ADOBE PHOTOSHOP

PHOTOSHOP AS A VIDEO EDITING TOOL? Who would have guessed it would become one back in 2003? When Adobe rolled out Photoshop CS, it introduced the application in two flavors, Regular and Extended. The Extended version of Photoshop came bearing gifts for those who work with video, 3D, and medical imaging. At the time, HDSLR video hadn't yet entered the scene, and the feature set was a bit light for the masses to jump in and start editing video.

Enter Photoshop CS6. With that release, Adobe completely overhauled the video features in Photoshop and made it possible for users to edit video on the software that they knew and loved. In fact, it's easy to use and more powerful than it appears at first glance.

This chapter will help you edit video in a creative and professional way without having to learn the entire world of video. You'll learn exactly what you need to do while building on your existing knowledge base. You'll also get your feet wet and learn the basics of getting footage into Photoshop and begin trimming and assembling your video.

Importing Your Footage

TIP Adobe has included video in both Photoshop Standard and Extended.

To begin editing your video footage, it's best to organize your Photoshop workspace so it is easy to work with your footage. Fortunately, there is a video workspace already set up with the most common tools you'll need. (If you're starting a new Photoshop project, choose Window > Workspace > Motion to set your workspace.) This workspace will contain most of the tools that you'll use to work with video and motion.

The Timeline is where all the magic happens. It is where you will perform all your timing and editing. In Photoshop, the Timeline is a component of the interface that chronologically displays your edited sequence in a linear fashion (**FIGURE 3.1**).

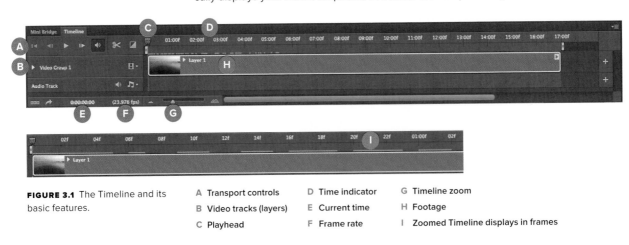

FIGURE 3.1 The Timeline and its basic features.

A Transport controls
B Video tracks (layers)
C Playhead
D Time indicator
E Current time
F Frame rate
G Timeline zoom
H Footage
I Zoomed Timeline displays in frames

In the next step-by-step section you'll learn how to import your footage so you may want to skip ahead a couple of pages to that section first so you can see the Timeline as shown in Figure 3.1. You'll perform a lot of your work in the Timeline, so make sure it is visible. If it's not, choose Window > Timeline. Figure 3.1 shows the basic functions of the Timeline:

- **Transport controls**. These controls work just like the controls on your DVD player. Stop/Play, Fast Forward, and Rewind should all be familiar terms.

- **Video tracks.** The video tracks stack like layers. The difference between video tracks and layers is that each track has a time duration measured on the time indicator.

- **Playhead**. This little guy indicates where the video is in time. As it moves across the Timeline, it displays a red hairline that indicates the currently visible portion of the video. You can drag the playhead manually to move to a different portion of the Timeline. You'll be doing that a lot during an edit.

- **Time indicator.** This is like a ruler, but rather than distance, it measures time. When the Timeline is contracted, it will display seconds, for example, 11:00f. When you're zoomed into the Timeline, you'll see the individual frames displayed.

- **Current time.** This indicates what time the playhead is currently on. Time is counted in frames, so one second is 24 frames (at 24 fps) and 11.23 would be 11 seconds and 23 frames.

- **Frame rate**. This is the native frame rate of the video. Think of 23.97 as 24 frames per second.

- **Timeline zoom**. This controls the magnification of the Timeline. It doesn't change the duration of the clip. Just like you zoom in and out of an image to make it easier to work with, you can do the same thing with the Timeline.

- **Footage.** This displays the footage, showing its duration and a preview.

If you read the previous chapter, you should have some kind of asset management system in place, and your footage should be on either a portable drive or a drive connected to your computer. Please don't edit off the CompactFlash card or thumb drive!

The great aspect about working with video in Photoshop is that you don't need to know all the video format jargon because Photoshop will capture all the settings from the clip that you bring in and set the frame rate, size, and pixel aspect ratio for you.

The dimension and frame rate of the video project will be set to the first piece of footage that you add to the Timeline. Photoshop also supports most of the formats used by DSLR and point-and-shoot cameras, such as MOV, MP4, H.264, AVC, and so on.

You don't need to know all of the terms and definitions listed here to edit video in Photoshop; however, each term is useful to know if you'll be working with video in any depth.

Frame rate. The frame rate indicates how many images are displayed per second. Video is typically displayed at 30 fps, and cinema is displayed at 24 fps. Many people use 24 fps to produce a "cinematic look." Technically, the frame rates are actually 29.97 and 23.97 frames per second (as a workaround for historical broadcast limitations). For simplicity sake, let's just use 30 fps and 24 fps from here on.

Codec (coder, decoder). Video is encoded, or compressed, into a codec. A codec allows for compressed video to stream over digital broadcast systems or over the Web and allows the information to fit onto discs due to its smaller file size. A codec ensures that the file size is as small as possible with good quality for smooth playback for the end user. Sometimes the term codec is used loosely to describe a video compression format.

Video compression format. A video compression format is the format that digital video is encoded to. Lossless formats maintain quality, which are good for working files because quality is more important than file size for this purpose. Lossy formats are smaller and more lightweight, making them ideal as delivery formats for content consumers to enjoy. Because they are lossy, a compromise is made with quality in order to bring the file size down. The current industry standard is a flavor of MP4 known as H.264. This is the format supported on all iOS devices and most other portable devices, as well as many websites. A video format is to video as a JPEG is to an image file.

Aspect ratio. You may have heard the term 16:9 (widescreen). This is the ratio (rectangular shape) of the final video. It means that for every 9 pixels in height, there are 16 pixels in width. The 16:9 format is used for HD television and many computers and portable devices. And it is the default HD setting for most video cameras (4:3 was the common format used before HD). Note that aspect ratio has nothing to do with the size of the screen or the resolution; it's merely the proportions used.

Pixel aspect ratio. Unlike photographs, which all have square pixels, video can consist of rectangular-shaped pixels, which are displayed as square by the viewing decoder. This is the reason subjects onscreen sometimes look "skinny." However, most DSLR cameras use square pixels. If you encounter non-square pixels in your video, you can display them as square in Photoshop by choosing View > Pixel Aspect Ratio and changing the menu to the appropriate pixel aspect ratio.

Common sizes. Video sizes are measured in height. The reason is that they used to be based on vertical rows of lines, and the widths could vary. Currently, the common sizes include:

- 1080 = 1080 pixels in height and 1920 pixels wide (Full HD)
- 720 = 720 pixels in height and 1280 pixels wide
- 480 NTSC = 480 pixels in height and 720 pixels wide
- 576 PAL (used in Asia and parts of Europe) = 576 pixels in height and 720 pixels wide
- 2k, 3k, 4k. These sizes are newer sizes and are 2000, 3000 and 4000 pixels, respectively

P(rogressive) or i(nterlaced)? Interlaced "fields" were an older way of compressing video for broadcast. Typically, the upper and lower fields were transmitted separately and played back quickly, so the eyes couldn't detect the flickering. However, you could see the scan lines in interlaced footage. Interlacing is being phased out as better technologies are coming to market.

Progressive compression, on the other hand, displays the entire image at once and uses lossy technology similar to JPEG to reduce the file size. Lossy technology compresses files by discarding redundant detail. When a video is compressed in high quality, the eye cannot see the difference in quality. However, a high-quality lossy file will have a larger file size than a low-quality lossy file. When too much compression is applied, the video can appear soft and display weird pixelated blocks, which are called *artifacts*. Good compression is a balancing act between file size and video quality.

Follow these steps to import your footage when you're starting a new Photoshop project or working in an existing one:

1. With the Motion workspace open, choose File > Open or click the plus button at the right side of the Timeline. I recommend letting the video clip define the size of the document. You can change the size later when you encode the video. If you have an existing Photoshop document you want to bring video into, choose Layer > Video Layers > New Video Layer from File.

2. From the files you downloaded for this book, navigate to the **footage** folder, select **edit_1.mp4**, which is a clip of the ocean, and click OK.

   Your video appears in the Timeline and in the Viewer, as shown in **FIGURE 3.2**.

CAUTION! Don't place the video into an existing document using the Place command, or the video will be placed as a Smart Object and treated like a graphic. As a result, you will lose many of the editing options.

FIGURE 3.2 The workspace with a video open in Photoshop.

Achieving Smooth Playback

View your video by clicking the Play button ▶ in the Transport controls or by pressing the spacebar to play or stop playback (click the Timeline first if this doesn't work).

You can move through the Timeline by "scrubbing" or click-dragging the playhead across the Timeline. The Timeline will also compress or expand when you move the slider directly under the beginning of the clip on the Timeline. When you expand or compress the Timeline, you aren't changing the speed of the video or altering it. You are just zooming in or out of the live area to help you edit with precision or gain a bird's-eye view of the Timeline.

You may notice some green markings on the Timeline that are displayed as a solid line or they may look like Morse code as the playback runs (**FIGURE 3.3**).

FIGURE 3.3 The green indicators show playback status.

The green markings indicate that you are playing back in real time and not missing any frames. As you play back the video, the video data is stored in the computer's RAM. As the video is cached (stored in RAM), green markings will appear on the Timeline. Depending on the performance of your machine and the amount of installed RAM, you may get real-time playback right away, or you may have to play the video once to load it (note that playback can appear jerky during this phase) and then play it back for a smoother view when the Timeline is green and loaded (this is called RAM preview).

If your machine can't keep up with the video, the video appears jerky and the audio might skip. If you want to hear the audio smoothly, right-click on the panel option menu at the right and choose Allow Frame Skipping. This option will configure Photoshop so it skips over video frames and enable smooth playback of the sound. Note that this option doesn't hinder the quality of the final video; it's just for previewing.

Trimming Clips

You'll promptly discover that people's attention span is short when they are viewing video. Also, you'll find that you can amass a lot of video very quickly. So, it's vital to trim your clips to the key moments of action according to your project.

1. Using the **edit_1.mp4** file from the previous section, trim your video by clicking on the edge of either end of the clip and dragging it toward the middle of the Timeline. A preview window allows you to view the video. While keeping a watchful eye on the preview, drag the beginning of the clip until you see the point that you want to cut. In the ocean video example, let's trim the clip at 2:16 when the water begins to come in (FIGURE 3.4).

FIGURE 3.4 Trimming the beginning of the clip.

2. Release the mouse to trim the clip. Notice that the edited clip snaps to the beginning of the Timeline (FIGURE 3.5). Although it appears that you have only this part of the clip preserved, the footage isn't deleted; it's only hidden. You can change the trim point at any time by simply clicking and dragging the head or tail of the clip again.

FIGURE 3.5 The trimmed footage.

A *slip edit* is when you keep the duration of a trimmed clip but move the position of the footage within it. For example, say you have a clip that is 30 seconds long. You trim 10 seconds from the head and 10 seconds from the tail of the clip. The result is a clip that is 10 seconds in duration that begins playing at 10 seconds and ends at 20 seconds. Now let's say that you want to keep the clip's timing on the Timeline, but you want to begin displaying the clip at 5 seconds and end it at 15 seconds. You will "slip" the trimmed footage 5 seconds, in essence moving the footage within the trim point. Do this by selecting the clip, pressing and holding the Option+Command (Alt+Ctrl) keys, and dragging to the left or right.

Let's trim the end of the clip too.

1. Click and drag the edge of the video track on the Timeline but begin from the end of the clip this time.

2. Drag until you see 8:00 as the duration at the top right of the preview window (**FIGURE 3.6**). Release to trim the clip to a total of 8 seconds.

FIGURE 3.6 Trimming the tail, or end, of the clip.

Adding Multiple Clips

If all your videos are just a single stream of activity, they will become boring very quickly. Many times you'll want to add multiple clips to the Timeline for variety. There are several ways to do this. Keep your current file open and follow these steps:

1. To add more clips to the Timeline, click the plus button to the right of the Timeline or click the Filmstrip icon on the left and choose Add Media to Timeline.

    This will open the Finder window for you to navigate to your footage.

2. Navigate to the **footage** folder that you downloaded for this book (see the Introduction for details).

3. Select multiple clips at once to save time. Choose **edit_2.mp4** (basketball players at the beach) and **edit_3.mp4** (cars that rack-focus to bokeh), as shown in **FIGURE 3.7**. I shot all three clips you are working with on the same day at Laguna Beach using a Canon 5D Mark II. I've reduced the size of the clips to make them easier to work with and not tax your computer's performance.

FIGURE 3.7 Choosing clips to add to the project.

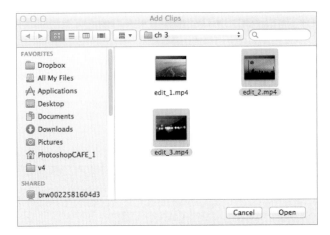

The clips will appear on the Timeline one after the other (**FIGURE 3.8**). The reason all the video clips are nicely arranged without gaps in between is because they are arranged inside a video group, which I'll discuss next.

FIGURE 3.8 Multiple clips on the Timeline that have also been loaded into layers.

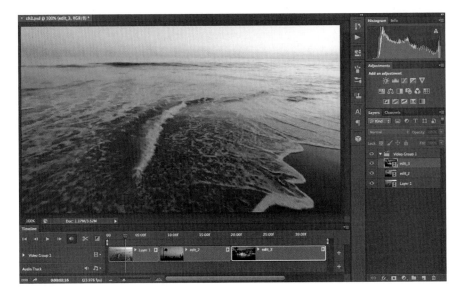

Changing the Order of Clips

A glance at the Layers panel reveals the video group that was created by adding multiple videos to the Timeline. A video group works exactly like a regular layer group in terms of functionality. However, what makes a video group so powerful goes beyond just mere organization. The brilliance is that every video in the group will appear on the Timeline on the same video track without gaps (see the "Ripple Edit" sidebar to learn more).

To change the order of the clips, you place the cursor over a clip and then click and drag it to another location in the Timeline, either before or after other clips. Notice that all the pieces on the video track snap to position, which is a wonderful feature that makes editing in Photoshop very easy. Drag the ocean clip and release it between the other two clips so you can experience reshuffling clips (FIGURE 3.9).

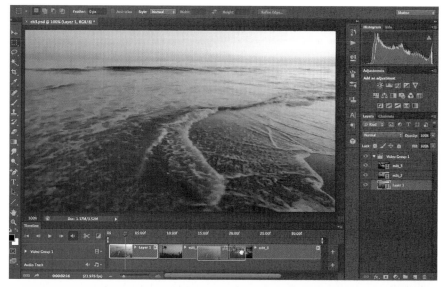

FIGURE 3.9 Drag a clip in the Timeline to change its order.

RIPPLE EDIT

When video editors trim and cut video, they use a technique called a *ripple edit*. Rippling means that when a clip is shortened or removed, all the gaps are closed up. If there are gaps, the video would play back with moments of nothingness, usually manifested as a black screen and silence. Some programs, such as Adobe Premiere Pro, come will ripple tools. Photoshop doesn't need ripple tools because all the clips inside the video group are automatically rippled.

You can also reposition clips within the video group, which is another handy feature and a lot easier too. In the Layers panel, notice that the clips are arranged chronologically from the bottom to the top. They are stacked from the bottom up, meaning that the bottom layer plays first and the top layer plays last.

To change the order of a clip, you can drag it up or down inside the video group in the Layers panel. As you do, notice that the clips' order changes in the Timeline (**FIGURE 3.10**).

For now, change your clips into this order: ocean, basketball players, cars.

FIGURE 3.10 Arranging multiple clips on the Timeline.

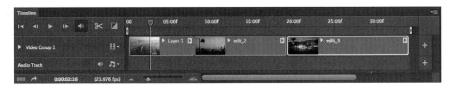

Assembling a Rough Cut

A *rough cut* (or assembly) is when you roughly trim the In and Out points of clips and arrange the clips in the correct order on the Timeline. The cuts don't have to be exact at this point. You just need to make sure all the content is there and in the correct order.

TIP If for any reason, you receive a "Cannot locate missing media" warning, read the "Saving and Managing Projects" section that follows to learn about relinking files.

1. Trim the additional clips in the Timeline by dragging the beginnings and ends of the clips. Be sure to capture the main action while minimizing the boring parts where nothing is happening.

   For example, trim the basketball shot after the player has taken the shot and his opponent has caught the rebound. The action is over at this point, so you don't need the extra footage afterward because it's not important to the story. Notice that the additional clips move to fill in the gaps.

   As you edit the clips, the audio and the video are trimmed together.

2. Save your project at this point and name it something memorable, such as "shortfilm_bball_beach." Everything you work on in Photoshop is saved as a PSD file.

You can view and compare my completed trimmed clip by opening the file **ch3-end.psd** file in the **Ch03** folder of files you downloaded for this book. **FIGURE 3.11** shows the current project state.

FIGURE 3.11 The saved project.

Saving and Managing Projects

When working on your projects, it's always a good idea to save your work as you go. But how are projects saved and managed in Photoshop? You save your file as a PSD file. The PSD contains all the trims, edits, text, graphics, and basically everything except the video footage and audio files. The video footage isn't embedded into the PSD; if it were, it would make for a huge file and cause potential problems and cause serious limitations for the length of videos.

The video is referenced in Photoshop. This means you choose a location to save the video files and Photoshop points to the original files when you place them into a project. Be careful if you decide to move the original video clips, though. You'll need to rename them or delete them, or else the references will be broken and you will see a "Cannot locate missing media" dialog when you open the Photoshop document (**FIGURE 3.12**).

FIGURE 3.12 This dialog appears to indicate that media is missing.

To reconnect media, it's a very simple process. You can try this with some of the exercise files that you downloaded for the book, although it's not always easily reproducible to break links so it might be better to keep this tip handy for when you need it.

1. Click the Choose button to the left of the name of the missing footage.

2. Navigate to the location of the video clip. Select the video clip and choose Open (**FIGURE 3.13**).

FIGURE 3.13 Navigate to the video clip to relink the footage.

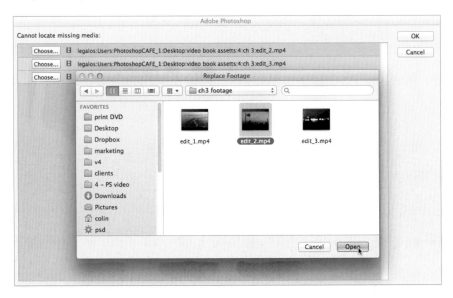

The footage will be linked and you will see a check box to the left of the footage name (**FIGURE 3.14**). If the other missing clips are in the same folder, they will automatically be updated too. Otherwise, you will need to click the Choose button for each clip and update the links.

FIGURE 3.14 The relinked and updated footage.

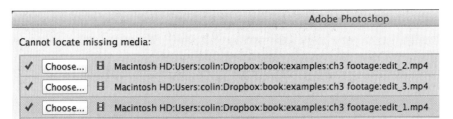

Editing an Interview

Interviews require a special approach to editing. In an interview, the audio plays a particularly important role. Sometimes the interviewee will stumble a lot and you'll want to fix those slipups. Oftentimes, other footage and images display as the speaker talks so viewers don't have to watch a talking head the whole time. At this point, the interviewer's role almost changes to that of a commentator.

The tool you'll use to fix these slipups is the Scissors tool . The Scissors tool allows you to split the video clip and remove a segment.

Follow these steps to fix some simple issues, such as um's and coughs, phones ringing, and other annoyances:

1. Open the **interview.mp4** file from the **footage** folder, or use your own video. Play the video and listen to the dialogue until you hear a section you want to remove—for example, a stumble over words, a cough, or a background noise. There is an um that can be edited out of the clip in the example footage. There is also a break between two thoughts by the interviewee, so there's a good place to cut at 15:12.

2. Select the clip to edit by either clicking on the layer in the Layers panel or selecting it on the Timeline.

3. Place the playhead exactly where you want to make the cut (**FIGURE 3.15**). Zoom into the clip for more precision when doing this kind of edit.

4. Click the Scissors tool in the Timeline (**FIGURE 3.16**). You will notice that the clip splits, or becomes divided at the playhead. The clip is now divided into two clips in the Layers panel and on the Timeline.

TIP Be careful that you don't overdo this part. You don't need to edit out each time the interviewee breathes, for example, because the video can start to become very choppy.

TIP When editing the audio, be careful to leave a little blank space between words, so the rhythm of the speech is consistent. Avoid editing too tightly.

FIGURE 3.15 The playhead parked at 15:12 on the interview project.

FIGURE 3.16 Splitting the clip in half by clicking the Scissors tool.

5. Move the playhead to the end of the segment you want to remove. Sadly, audio scrubbing isn't supported, so you will have to play back the video to hear it. If you are cutting a large portion, it may serve you well to zoom out of the Timeline a bit. Move the Playhead to 17 seconds.

6. Click the Scissors tool a second time. After making another cut, you will see an additional clip in the Layers panel (**FIGURE 3.17**).

FIGURE 3.17 Making a second cut.

7. Select the section that has been cut and press the Delete key to remove the offending portion (**FIGURE 3.18**). Ripple magic will happen again and the gap will be filled nicely.

FIGURE 3.18 To remove a section of the clip, select it and press Delete on the keyboard.

TIP When editing an interview, don't be too concerned about the appearance of the footage at this point. What really matters is what's being said. Make sure you trim and assemble the footage so the dialogue flows nicely. Storytelling is key here.

8. Move the playhead back a couple of seconds and preview the trim to make sure you didn't cut off half a word. You can fine-tune the trim by clicking and dragging at the ends of the clips.

9. Move the playhead to 22:17 where there is another break in thought. First, select the clip to cut by clicking on it. Then click the Scissors tool to split the selected clip into two (**FIGURE 3.19**). You should now have three clips.

FIGURE 3.19 Make a third cut at 22:17. Each cut creates a new layer and incrementally names each clip.

10. Trim off any excess at the end of the clip. If you preview the rest of the clips, there is some silence and then you hear "cut." Drag the end back to 33:20 to trim off the excess (**FIGURE 3.20**).

11. If you want, you can separate the clips on the Timeline. Drag the last clip to the right and it will break out of its ripple behavior (**FIGURE 3.21**). Drag the middle clip to the left a bit, too, to make some space between the clips on the Timeline. (This is in preparation for moving them to another timeline when we do more cutting in the next chapter.)

TIP When shooting an interview, it's a great idea to always leave 3 seconds of silence at the beginning and 3 seconds of silence at the end before stopping the recording. This provides a little headroom for editing.

FIGURE 3.20 Trimming the end of the video clip to remove excess footage.

12. Save the file and give it a meaningful name. A copy of it is saved in the **Ch03** folder for you to examine as **3-interview-end.psd**.

FIGURE 3.21 Separating the clips on the Timeline.

When cutting audio, you can always mask the visible appearance of cuts by using cutaways in the form of overlaying photos or other B-roll footage. B-roll is any footage that shows interesting action that isn't coming from the commentator. The great thing about B-roll is that, generally, you don't have to shoot it at the same time you conduct the interview. When you do shoot the B-roll, this is your opportunity to capture those beautiful wide shots or close, intimate shots with a shallow depth of field.

It's common to create cutaways of B-roll overlays for visual interest while the person is talking. This serves more than one purpose. It keeps it visually interesting, so the viewer isn't just looking at a talking head the entire time, and it helps strengthen the story. This technique also adds a nice commentary to the captured action footage. We will be cutting this B-roll in the next chapter.

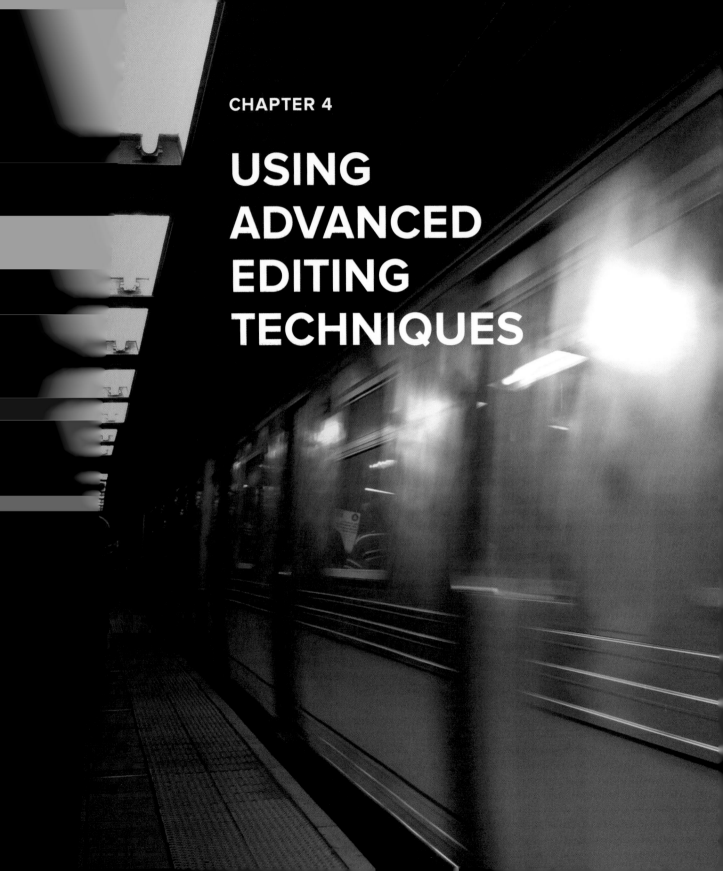

CHAPTER 4

USING ADVANCED EDITING TECHNIQUES

AT THIS POINT YOU'VE LEARNED SOME OF THE EDITING BASICS of importing, trimming, and moving footage. But there is so much more that you can do with video in Photoshop. Throughout the rest of the book you'll learn about all kinds of features and techniques. This chapter is the first step of that discovery process.

Here you'll start to add the cool effects that make your videos look more polished. You will learn about multi-track editing, how layers and Blend modes work with video, and how to mix different types of media on a Timeline. But don't worry; the learning curve is not difficult.

Transitions

Transitions help you create a smooth change between different clips of footage. You may have noticed in the footage that you've cut so far that the transitions are jarring. The video plays from one clip and then jumps to the next one. A nice cross dissolve transition would make this shift a little smoother. The good news is that Photoshop makes it very easy to apply this kind of effect. There are five different types of transitions in Photoshop:

■ **Fade.** This effect fades the footage to transparency over time. It is ideal to use if the clip is stacked on top of another clip.

■ **Cross Fade.** This effect creates a smooth blending fade with the adjacent clip on the Timeline.

■ **Fade With Black.** This effect fades the clip to or from a solid black color

■ **Fade With White.** This effect fades the clip to or from a solid white color.

■ **Fade With Color.** This effect fades the clip to or from a customized color. When you click this transition, a color swatch appears at the lower right of the panel for you to choose a color you want to use.

The *Duration* option determines the span of time that the transition will appear. A short duration will produce a more sudden change, whereas a longer duration will create a smooth, slow change. The number you enter in the Duration box will be the default timing for all transitions when they are applied.

Applying Transition Effects

Let's add some transitions to the footage you were working with in Chapter 3:

1. Open the project **ch4.psd** (either your saved project file so far, or the one I have provided for you in the download that comes with this book in the **ch4** folder). This is where you left off with the beach scene in the previous chapter (**FIGURE 4.1**).

TIP Although we have step-by-step instructions with the provided footage, feel free to substitute your own footage once you are comfortable with the steps. This is the best way for you to learn and retain what you have learned.

FIGURE 4.1 The project is opened and ready to add transitions to.

FIGURE 4.2 Click the button to open the Transitions window.

2. Click the Transitions button at the left of the Timeline to open the Transitions panel and see a list of available transitions (**FIGURE 4.2**).

3. Click the Fade option, and change the default transition time to 2 seconds either by clicking the triangle and dragging the slider or by simply typing **2** in the Duration field (**FIGURE 4.3**). All transitions applied will now be 2 seconds long by default until you enter a different value in the Duration field.

4. To apply a transition, drag the transition you desire from the Transitions panel and drop it on the Timeline at the beginning or end of a clip you want to affect. If you want to apply a Fade effect (as in this example), drop it where the two clips meet (**FIGURE 4.4**).

TIP When you change the transition time in the Transitions panel, it doesn't matter which transition type is selected because all the defaults will be changed to the new value.

FIGURE 4.3 Change the Duration value of the transition in the Transitions panel.

TIP If for any reason, you receive a "Cannot locate missing media" warning, read the "Saving and Managing Projects" section in Chapter 3 to learn about relinking files.

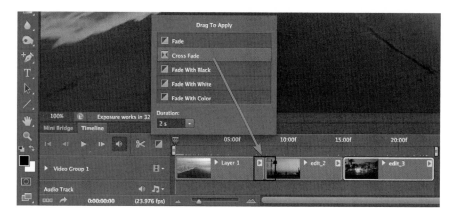

FIGURE 4.4 Apply a transition effect.

5. Apply a Fade transition between the second and third clip, too. Click the Play button (or press the spacebar) to play the video to see how the transitions affect the video (FIGURE 4.5).

FIGURE 4.5 The transitions in action.

6. Try a different type of transition. Drag a Fade With Black transition to the end of the Timeline, as shown in FIGURE 4.6. You may have to adjust the Timeline magnification slider or scroll the bottom scroll bar to see the end of the clips on the Timeline. When you view the video now, it will fade to black at the end. This is a common way to end a video; it's elegant and really gives viewers the impression of closure.

FIGURE 4.6 Applying a Fade With Black transition effect.

Modifying Transition Effects

After you've applied a transition to a clip, you can easily modify it. You can change the timing of the transition or the type of transition, or choose to remove the transition entirely.

1. Select the transition on the Timeline by clicking on it (FIGURE 4.7). A rectangle with two triangles appears.

FIGURE 4.7 Select the transition on the Timeline.

2. Drag the edge of the transition to change the duration. As you drag you'll see a display telling you the new duration. Continue to drag to make the transition shorter or longer (**FIGURE 4.8**).

3. To more precisely change the duration or to access more options, right-click on the transition (**FIGURE 4.9**):

■ Change the Duration by moving the slider which appears as soon as you click the triangle or by typing in a new number.

■ Click the drop-down menu next to the transition name and choose a different type of transition.

■ Click the trash can icon to remove the transition.

FIGURE 4.9 The transition options on the Timeline.

Adjusting Video Speed and Duration

You know you love it! What am I talking about? Slow motion. Picture this dramatic scene: A bride slowly turns to face the audience with a huge smile on her face. Hand in hand with her new husband as they walk out the door of the church, confetti falls, hands are clapping, radiant smiles are everywhere, and soft music plays. There is something about slowing down the action of such a scene that just completes it.

The drama that comes with slow motion isn't just related to romance. If you've ever seen sports in slow motion, you know that it allows you to see everything that happens and really appreciate the skills of the athletes. Any way you want to look at it, changing the speed of video has a way of connecting with your viewers in an emotional way.

For the best possible slow motion, set your camera to start shooting at a higher frame rate and then slow it down to the equivalent of a normal 24 or 30 fps when you are editing in Photoshop. For example, some cameras allow you to shoot at a speed of 60 fps.

When you play back a 60 fps video at the usual 30 fps, you'll have perfect quality video at 50 percent of the normal speed. Editing the speed also changes the duration of the action (60/30 = 2 seconds of footage for every second of captured footage).

Fortunately, even if you don't possess a camera capable of shooting at 60 or 120 fps, you can still create great slow motion. Photoshop does an excellent job of interpolating the frames and playing back the video at different speeds with decent quality.

Slowing down the video action using Photoshop

Let's continue with the project you've been working on (ch4.psd) and slow down the scene of the basketball players to 50 percent speed. Half speed may not sound like a lot, but you'll be surprised by the effect that it has.

1. Scrub the playhead until you see the basketball clip. Choose the desired basketball action clip by clicking on it in the Timeline.

2. Right-click to display a Settings dialog with two options: Duration and Speed (FIGURE 4.10).

FIGURE 4.10 The Duration and Speed options in the Timeline.

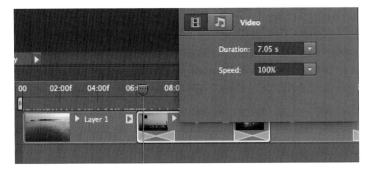

FIGURE 4.11 Changing the Duration and Speed options in the Timeline.

3. You want slow motion, so change the settings for speed to 50 and type in **14** for the duration (FIGURE 4.11). See the sidebar to understand why we changed the duration.

SPEED AND DURATION

To slow down the speed of the playback, you need to choose a smaller number. If you want to speed it up, choose a number larger than 100%. You want half speed for the basketball scene, so you change the setting to 50% for Speed. There could be a slight problem here. If the footage is slowed down to half speed and the duration is the same, you will only get part of the clip. That means that the clip will stop playing before the player even shoots the basket. This is the reason that Duration is also in the Settings dialog. If you slow the speed by half, you need to compensate by increasing the duration of the clip. If you want to show the same portion of the clip, you need to double the duration. How do you figure this out? Simple; you divided the speed by 2, so you balance it by multiplying the duration by 2. This is simple math; whatever you do for one setting, you do the opposite to the other to maintain balance.

4. Play back the video. It looks great in slow motion. If you need to further adjust the duration, click on the edge of the clip at the beginning or end and drag to change it. Notice that there is no sound now. When you change the duration of a clip, you lose the audio. You'll fix the audio by masking it in Chapter 5, "Bringing Video Alive With Sound."

5. The transitions might also have been affected by the speed changes. Right-click on each transition to check its speed. The first one changed to .5 seconds, as you can see in **FIGURE 4.12**, and the second one changed to 4 seconds. Right-click and type in **2** seconds for each one. If the speed of your transitions didn't change, great!

6. Play back the video again just to make sure it plays the way you want it to (**FIGURE 4.13**).

FIGURE 4.12 Fixing the transition speed.

FIGURE 4.13 Playing back the video to check the speed and transitions.

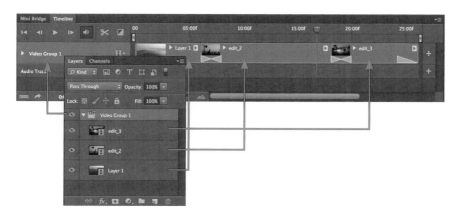

Working with Multiple Video Tracks

Video groups are a very useful way of keeping video clips together in a linear fashion. **FIGURE 4.14** shows a video group and how the Layers panel maps to the Timeline. Whenever you import video, a video group will automatically be created. Put simply, a video group is in fact a video track.

FIGURE 4.14 A video group and how the Timeline matches the Layers panel.

TIP If you prefer to populate a new video group with a clip, select the clip first. Then choose the option New Video Group from Clips and the selected clip will be moved to the new group.

For the majority of editing purposes, using a single video track is sufficient. But when you need to be a bit more creative, you'll need to work with more than one video track. The advantage of stacking video layers is that whatever you can do with images in layers, most of the time you can do the same thing with video layers. For example, you can apply layer opacity and Blend modes with video to create great-looking effects. To stack the clips on top of each other, you first need to split a Timeline into more than one track. Let's walk through the process step by step.

1. Click the Filmstrip icon at the right of Video Group 1 on the Timeline. On the menu that appears, choose New Video Group (FIGURE 4.15).

FIGURE 4.15 Options to create a new video group.

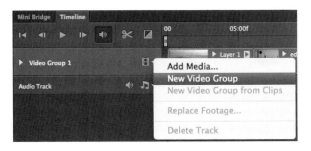

A new empty video group called Video Group 2 will be created above the existing group (FIGURE 4.16).

FIGURE 4.16 Video Group 2 is ready for footage.

2. With a new video group created, it's easy to move clips into it. Just drag your clips from other groups into the new group. Using the example files (FIGURE 4.17), drag the ocean clip into Video Group 2.

    Notice that the clip moves to the new group and the rest of the footage nudges to the left to fill in the gap (FIGURE 4.18).

FIGURE 4.17 Click and drag a clip into the desired video group. You can then stack video.

FIGURE 4.18 A multitrack video project.

To more quickly move a clip onto a new track, from the Layers panel select the clip that is currently residing in a video group and drag it up in the layer stack. I call this *jail breaking* the clip from the group. Drag it above the video group until you see a line appear above the group (FIGURE 4.19). As simple as it sounds and looks, it requires a little practice.

Release the clip. It will then be in its own group (track) located above the original group (FIGURE 4.20, LEFT). Notice that there are now two video tracks in the Timeline and in the Layers panel (FIGURE 4.20, RIGHT). When there is only one video clip, it doesn't have to be encased in a group; it will perform the same function as a video layer.

FIGURE 4.19 Jail break a clip by dragging it out of the video group.

FIGURE 4.20 The Timeline matches the Layers panel.

Using Blend Modes

When it comes to creative tools, Photoshop has a plethora of them. One of the best tools for making layers look great when they are stacked on each other is a Blend mode. Blend modes influence the way that layers interact. Different Blend modes produce various results. A favorite tool of compositors and collage artists, Blend modes are also very useful for video, too. They make it easy for you to create that wow effect with your videos.

Each Blend mode changes the way that a layer reacts with the layer underneath it. You can get a small inkling of how a Blend mode affects a clip by adjusting the opacity of a layer. Using Blend modes opens up an entirely new world. A technical explanation of each Blend mode is provided in Photoshop's Help menu. Don't get too caught up in the Blend mode definitions. What matters is how they look in your video, and the best way to determine this is to experiment with them.

TIP To easily see what all the Blending modes look like on your layer, click the Move tool. Then press Shift+ to cycle through all the Blend modes one at a time. Press Shift+− to cycle backward.

Working with Blend Modes

To use a layer Blend mode, you need to have a document with at least two layers. At the top of the Layers panel is an option called Normal. Click the drop-down menu next to Normal to see all the available modes (FIGURE 4.21).

You change a layer's Blend mode by first selecting the layer. Then click the drop-down menu and choose one of the Blend modes to view the result in your document window.

BLEND MODE CATEGORIES

It's beyond the scope of this book to explain each Blend mode. Actually, it would be boring and pointless because what matters is the effect of the Blend modes. There are six categories (FIGURE 4.22), and each mode is a variation of its group:

- **Normal.** No special blending takes place; only opacity affects these layers.

- **Darken.** The result darkens the image. White is invisible on the blend layer.

- **Lighten.** The result lightens the image. Black is invisible on the blend layer.

- **Contrast.** Increases contrast; 50% gray is invisible on the blend layer.

- **Comparative.** The difference between images is apparent.

- **Color.** Works on different color qualities.

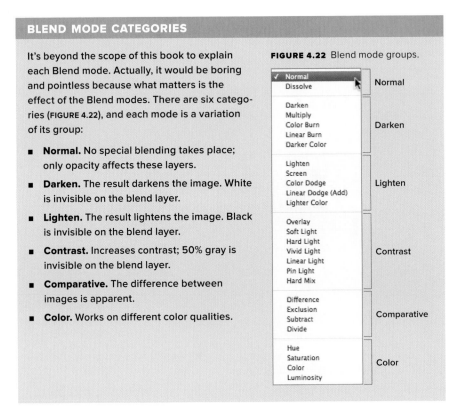

FIGURE 4.22 Blend mode groups.

Let's add a little something to the current project (**ch4.psd**) you are working on using the Blend modes:

1. Choose the layer with the ocean on it.

2. Change the Blend mode to Overlay. Scrub through the video and notice the result of blending two layers of video together (FIGURE 4.23). It looks like a more complex effect than it actually is, and it's lots of fun! Try applying various modes to your layers. You may like a different one better.

3. Feel free to experiment with the opacity of the top layer, too, by changing its setting in the Layers panel. My preference is an Opacity of 90% (FIGURE 4.24), but choose what looks best to you.

FIGURE 4.23 The layer Blend mode is changed to Overlay.

FIGURE 4.24 Drop the Opacity to 90% for a better-looking result.

Adding Polish to the Video

Even though the project you're working on is looking good, there are more transitions and tweaks you can make to further enhance it.

For example, notice that the top layer drops off without a transition. This is a great time in the video to use the Fade transition. The fade will increase the transparency, which will nicely blend the top track into the footage when it ends.

FIGURE 4.25 Create a Fade transition.

1. Click the Transition button, and then drag the Fade transition to the end of the video track on the ocean (the top video track) (**FIGURE 4.25**).

   The transition looks good, but the clip seems to end too soon. Recall that editing is nondestructive and merely hides the trimmed video. This is a great time to bring back some of the hidden parts of the video.

2. Click the end of the top video layer and drag it to the right. Release the layer just after the end of the basketball players underneath to place the transitions on top of each other (**FIGURE 4.26**).

FIGURE 4.26 Extending the length of the top track.

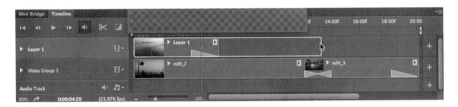

All the clips now blend nicely at the same time. It's a very smooth, good-looking effect (**FIGURE 4.27**). Don't be afraid to make tweaks mid project like you did here by extending the top video track. If you see that your video can be improved in some way, do it!

FIGURE 4.27 The results of the transition; all the videos fade together.

To finesse the visual appeal of the cuts, let's add some Fade With Black transitions.

3. Choose the Fade With Black transition and drag it to the beginning of each track. If you only add it to one track, the effect won't affect both tracks, so you need to repeat the transition for each track (FIGURE 4.28).

4. Save your project and name it ch4-end.psd so that you can continue to use it in later chapters.

(To view the completed project, open **ch4-end.psd** in the **ch4** folder. You may have to re-link the footage.)

As you saw in this chapter, you can create some appealing effects with layered video clips. The fun has only just begun, so keep reading.

Combining Two Video Documents

So far you have created a series of stacked videos with transitions. You also cut up a basic interview at the end of the last chapter. In this section, you are going to combine the two together to start to tell a story and finesse the video's timing and sequence. In the next steps, you'll combine footage from a beach scene with an interview.

1. Open **interview.psd** from the **ch4** folder in your downloaded files.

2. Rename Video Group 1 as **interview** as shown in FIGURE 4.29. It's important to have unique names for video groups; otherwise, you won't be able to copy them to another document that has a group with the same name. Leave this document open.

FIGURE 4.28 Adding a Fade With Black transition effect to polish the project.

FIGURE 4.29 Rename the video group and collapse it by clicking the triangle by its name in the Layers panel.

TIP If for any reason, you receive a "Cannot locate missing media" warning, read the "Saving and Managing Projects" section in Chapter 3 to learn about relinking files.

3. Now open **ch4-end.psd** from the **Ch4** folder (or use the file you were working on in the previous steps). Place the playhead on frame one. You should see a blank Video Group2. If not, create a new blank video group by clicking on the filmstrip to the right of the Timeline name and choosing New Video Group.

4. Click on the blank video group to select it as shown in **FIGURE 4.30**. The transferred clips will go into this group.

FIGURE 4.30 Make sure a blank video group is selected at the top of the Timeline.

5. Choose Window > Arrange > 2-up Vertical. You will now see both document windows side by side in Photoshop as shown in **FIGURE 4.31**.

FIGURE 4.31 Splitting the window view into two panes.

6. Click the Interview document's tab at the top to activate it. Click the interview Video Group icon in the Layers panel. Shift-drag the icon into the second window (**FIGURE 4.32**). Pressing the Shift key ensures that the video clips are properly centered in the destination document.

FIGURE 4.32 Dragging the contents of one document into another.

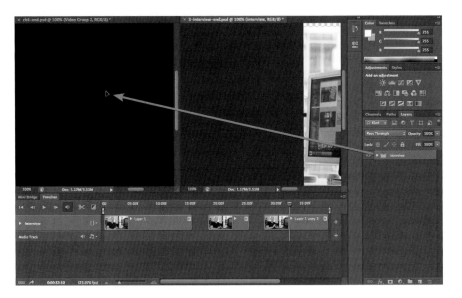

 **TIP** In the real world, I might have built all of these assets into the same document. The reason I built them separately and then joined the projects is so that you can learn this as a possible workflow. For example, you might have different people collaborating on a project in a pipeline workflow. Or, perhaps the file is too big and getting bogged down, so you build the parts separately and then put them together to preserve system resources.

7. Release the mouse and the clips from the interview are added to the Timeline of the ch4-end.psd document.

Close the original interview document as it's not needed anymore. Your screen should look like **FIGURE 4.33**.

FIGURE 4.33 The clips from the interview are added to the working project.

Editing an Interview with Footage

Now that you have the interview footage combined with the beach material, it's a matter of arranging and massaging things around. I'll show you a few tricks that help make a decent interview cut. There will also be a few workarounds that you can employ to make Photoshop do what's needed.

In addition, you're going to add a photograph as a slide to add some visual interest to the presentation. It will also show you that we can work with many types of animated media in Photoshop.

You should have a file of combined interview and beach footage from the steps in the previous section.

1. Click on the filmstrip on the left of the Timeline and choose New Video Group from the menu (**FIGURE 4.34**). If new video group is not at the top of the stack, drag it to the top by either dragging the Video Track name in the Timeline or in the Layers panel.

FIGURE 4.34 Creating a new video group.

2. Click the Plus button on the right of the Timeline to add media. Navigate to the **Ch4** folder of your downloaded files and choose **pic-beach-sunset2.jpg**. Click Open (**FIGURE 4.35**).

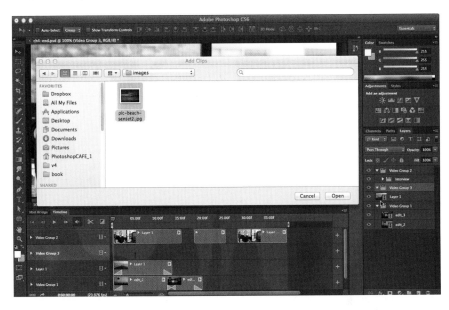

3. Begin to drag some of the clips around to arrange things. The first clip of the interview goes all the way to the left. (If you want, trim the beginning slightly as there is a couple seconds of silence.)

Select all three video clips of the beach shots. Command/Ctrl-click to select multiple clips. Drag those clips to the right, toward the end of the first interview clip as you see in **FIGURE 4.36**.

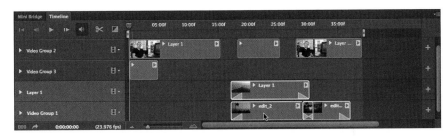

4. Drag the photo clip toward the end of the first interview clip and expand it if necessary by dragging on the edge of the clip to make it last about 5 seconds (**FIGURE 4.37**).

5. Play the video through a few times, adjusting the timing of the interview clips and the clips underneath until the timing feels good (**FIGURE 4.38**). Take the visibility of the last two interview clips to zero by adjusting the opacity in the Layers panel.

   If you want to adjust a clip, don't forget to place the playhead over it.

   By reducing the opacity, you can keep the audio playing for those clips but allow the imagery to show from underneath instead of the talking head.

TIP Why did we reduce the opacity of the videos rather than hide them by turning off their layer visibility (by clicking the eye icons)? If you turn off layer visibility, it also mutes the audio. If you want to hear only the audio and hide the clips, reduce the layer opacity to zero.

FIGURE 4.38 Setting the timing for all the clips.

6. Before we finish the project, let's add one little extra piece of visual goodness and animate the slide using a Timeline effect. I'll spare you the explanation here because we go deep into this in Chapter 8, "Creating Engaging Multimedia Slideshows." Right-click/Ctrl-click the Purple photo clip to display a Motion window. Choose Pan as the Motion Preset and click away to apply it (**FIGURE 4.39**). Now when you play the Timeline, you'll see there is a nice motion effect on the photograph that adds to the sizzle.

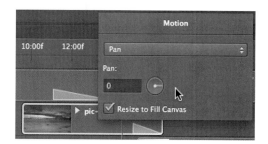

FIGURE 4.39 Adding a Motion Preset to the photograph.

7. **FIGURE 4.40** shows the final adjusted Timeline. Notice that you have added a fade transition to the first interview. I have also added a fade transition to the photograph so that it fades gently into the video footage.

FIGURE 4.40 The final project so far. Look at the Layers panel and the Timeline to make sure your document matches.

8. Open **ch4-interview-end.psd** from the **Ch4** folder to see the final result.

In this chapter, we've covered a lot of ground as far as more advanced editing goes. You still need to work on color, adjustments, filters, and sound to complete the project, but we'll turn to adjusting footage in the next chapter.

CHAPTER 5

BRINGING VIDEO ALIVE WITH SOUND

SOUND IS THE SECRET SAUCE to successful video productions. Turn the sound off while watching a movie and you instantly notice the amount of impact that gets lost. Music sets the mood, background sounds provide clues to the location, and dialogue helps tell the story. Don't ignore sound—it's very important in your productions. This chapter explores the audio options in Photoshop.

The Basics of Audio in Photoshop

Though not an audio editing program per se, Photoshop can do a few useful things with audio. The feature set is easy to learn, and it offers enough tools for you to bring your video projects to life with sound. Here are just a few things you can do:

- Play audio on video tracks

- Add multiple tracks of audio and music

- Mix volume

- Mute audio tracks

- Fade sound in and out

These tasks are all covered in the pages ahead. However, let me first address the elephant in the room: For those who are serious about audio, don't throw away your digital audio workstation (DAW) just yet. Photoshop cannot sweeten audio, normalize sound, or reduce noise. You will need separate audio software for that; see the sidebar "Top Software for Editing Audio" for some suggestions.

Capturing Audio

One way to get sound for a production is to record it. Following are a few tips for recording audio and the tools commonly used:

- **External mics:** While you can use the built-in microphone on your camera, it's not usually the best option. If that's all you have, however, then go ahead and use it. Plugging in an external microphone is a better way to capture audio. If necessary, these mics can be hidden in props such as flower pots on tables so that they are hidden from viewers of your video.

- **Lav mics:** You can use handheld microphones for interviews, although lavalier mics are more commonly used because they can be positioned close to the speaker's mouth to minimize background noise. Lav mics, which are generally clipped to the shirt of the interviewee, come in wired and wireless configurations. Wireless is easier to manage because you don't have to hide any unsightly cables. Productions at PhotoshopCAFE use the Sennheiser wireless lavalier microphones for in-studio and location shooting. This microphone was also used for the mock interview clip used in these exercises.

- **Shotgun mics:** Shotgun microphones are very powerful and have a very narrow range of capture. These are aimed at interviewees' or actors' mouths and used to capture speech that is off-camera.

- **Boom:** On shoots, it's common to see an assistant with a microphone on a stick. This is called a boom, and it allows the sound engineer to get the microphone as close to the action as possible without having it show up in the scene.

- **Windsock:** A windsock, or pop filter, is a microphone cover used to eliminate the sound of wind hitting the microphone or plosives from the mouth. Windsocks range from foam that covers the diaphragm of the microphone to a "dead cat," the name given to those furry coverings you see. I have even stretched a stocking over a coat hanger to reduce the popping sound that comes from wind.

- **External preamp:** If you use the camera to manage the audio, I recommend using an external preamp between the microphone and the camera. The preamp interfaces with a high-quality microphone (it supports XLR cables, which aren't supported on most DSLR cameras), boosts the signal, and allows the camera to record a stronger and cleaner signal than by plugging directly into the camera. One affordably priced unit that I used on the project in the tutorial is called the JuicedLink (www.juicedlink.com) and can be seen in FIGURE 5.1.

FIGURE 5.1 A JuicedLink Riggy.

Capturing Dual Sound

Using *dual sound* is common in HDSLR audio. With dual sound, a separate device, such as a recorder by the manufacturer Zoom, is used to capture the audio. The audio is then mixed together with the video after the fact. The separate device features a better audio processing chip and a larger XLR input, which produces a better quality microphone than the on-camera microphone and results in less noise.

For most postproduction workflows, you mute the camera sound on the Timeline and align the audio to the track to play the higher quality sound from the external device. This is a common workflow when using Adobe Premiere Pro and Apple Final Cut along with a third-party plug-in called PluralEyes.

You can accomplish dual sound in Photoshop, but it's a trial-and-error process because there are no tools for syncing the audio sources in Photoshop. Instead, you nudge the audio around until it lines up. You can, however, use things like the clicking sound of a slate or even the clapping of hands to create a sync point. This gives you both a visual and an audible cue point.

TOP SOFTWARE FOR EDITING AUDIO

A number of dedicated applications do a great job of advanced audio editing. If you need to change bass and treble, reduce noise, take out pops, and generally clean up and sweeten your audio, look at using a DAW. This short list includes some of the top DAWs, ranging from free to pro, that are used for recording music albums and movie soundtracks (FIGURE 5.2).

- Adobe Audition: www.adobe.com/audition
- Audacity: audacity.sourceforge.net
- Apple Logic Pro: www.apple.com/logicpro
- Apple GarageBand: www.apple.com/garageband
- Sony ACID Pro: www.sonycreativesoftware.com/acidpro
- AVID Pro Tools: www.avid.com/US/products/family/pro-tools
- Roland Cakewalk: www.cakewalk.com
- REAPER: www.reaper.fm
- Cubase: www.steinberg.net/cubase
- Ableton Live: www.ableton.com

FIGURE 5.2 The Mixer in Adobe Audition.

Audio Settings in Photoshop

While Photoshop may lack a lot of features, such as panning and tone controls, it gives you control over the basic properties of audio tracks that you need to put a project together. Bear in mind that the audio settings are clip based, which means that the changes are applied only to the selected clip, not the entire track. This actually offers more freedom and options than would be available on a track-based system.

When you Ctrl-click/right-click either a video or an audio track, the same controls display (**FIGURE 5.3**). Graphics clips do not have an audio option, but you will learn to solve that problem in this chapter.

To access the audio settings on a clip, Ctrl-click/right-click the clip on the video Timeline (**FIGURE 5.4**). Opening the options on a video track first reveals video options such as speed and duration. Click the music note button at the top left of the options panel to reveal the audio options.

FIGURE 5.3 The audio options on a video track.

■ **Volume:** This controls the loudness of the audio. It can be used to boost the volume or reduce the volume of a track.

■ **Fade In:** This causes the music to ramp up over time. It starts with silence and evenly increases over time until it reaches the amount set in the Volume slider.

TIP Audio works on a clip-by-clip basis. If you want to adjust the audio mid-track, consider splitting the track.

■ **Fade Out:** The opposite of Fade In, the music starts at the maximum volume set and evenly decreases until it's silent. You have no doubt heard many songs on the radio that fade out at the end; this is the same effect.

■ **Mute:** Turns the audio on or off for the clip it's associated with.

FIGURE 5.4 The audio options on the Timeline.

Working with Audio in Photoshop

Now that it's clear what Photoshop can and can't do with sound, you can get to work. You'll start with the file **Ch5-start.psd**, which is the same file we finished in Chapter 4. Try wearing a set of over-the-ear headphones while editing audio for a more accurate monitoring system. The reason it's more accurate is because each room produces a different type of acoustic quality. Softer hollow spaces amplify bass, whereas hard surfaces cause echo (called reverberation, or reverb for short). The headphones cut out the ambient acoustics and allow you to concentrate on the actual sounds without distractions.

Adding Sound from Video

Open **Ch5-start.psd** (**FIGURE 5.5**) from the **Ch5** folder. Play back the video and notice that when the photograph cuts in, the sounds drop out to nothing. That's because it's in-between the speaking part and the cutaway of the ocean scene with the basketball players. The speaking part has sound and so does the cutaways, but the photo has nothing. To eliminate the awkward silence, and add the sound of the ocean without stacking another video track, follow these steps.

FIGURE 5.5 The Ch5-start.psd project is ready for you to pick right up from the last chapter and work with the sound.

TIP If for any reason, you receive a "Cannot locate missing media" warning, read the "Saving and Managing Projects" section in Chapter 3 to learn about relinking files.

1. If you open a video clip into an audio track, the video is stripped out and the audio remains. Click the music note next to the audio track, and then select Add Audio as shown in **FIGURE 5.6**.

2. Navigate to the video clip **edit-1.mp4** in the **footage** folder (**FIGURE 5.7**). Click OK to add the footage to the Audio track.

FIGURE 5.6 Adding audio to the track.

FIGURE 5.7 Choose a video clip to borrow its audio.

Notice in **FIGURE 5.8** that the audio track is displayed on the Timeline as a green bar. It's very cool that you can pull the audio track directly off a video clip without having to do anything else.

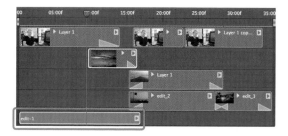

FIGURE 5.8 The audio track on the Timeline.

3. Shorten the duration of the sound clip by dragging from the left edge toward the right. You will notice that the clip snaps to the beginning of the Timeline. Once it snaps, click and drag the clip to the right and place it directly under the photograph as shown in **FIGURE 5.9**. Tweak it and play with the trim as necessary to mask the silence with the sound of waves on the beach—very fitting for this imagery.

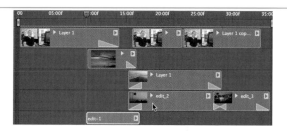

FIGURE 5.9 Trimming and positioning the audio track.

FIGURE 5.10 Making adjustments to the audio track.

4. Ctrl-click/right-click the audio track and change the settings according to **FIGURE 5.10**. Drop the overall Volume down to 60% so the sound is a little more subtle and not overriding other things. Set the Fade In and Fade Out to 2 seconds. This will make the sound slowly blend with the rest of the sound and not create an abrupt change. Play back the clip a few times and make edits as you see fit to create a smooth result.

Adding Music to a Video Project

I don't need to tell you that there is nothing like music to set a mood. Music has the ability to change the atmosphere, alter the mood, and transport the viewer to a different place or time. The power of music—as expressions of patriotism, political views, romance, victory, and much more—is evident throughout history. In the case of video, music is an awesome tool in the hands of a skilled editor. Follow these steps to add some music.

1. First, create a new track for the music. Click the music note on the audio track on the Timeline, and then select New Audio Track. Just like videos, you cannot stack sound files on top of each other without creating a new track (**FIGURE 5.11**).

    A brand-new track is added to the bottom of the Timeline. If you need to, scroll down the Timeline to see it as shown in **FIGURE 5.12**.

FIGURE 5.11 Creating a new audio track. Photoshop lets you add more audio tracks than you will ever need!

FIGURE 5.12 Two audio tracks on the Timeline.

TIP This is one of the many award-winning, licensed tracks through Triple Scoop Music (triplescoopmusic.com), which is a great source for finding quality music to bolster productions.

2. Click the music note and select Add Audio. Navigate to the **music** folder from your download to select the music track for the song "Rescue Me," an original score by artist Michael Burns provided with permission (**FIGURE 5.13**).

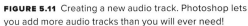

FIGURE 5.13 Selecting a song to add to the Timeline.

3. The music track is added to the Timeline as a green strip (**FIGURE 5.14**). Notice the song is much longer than the rest of the project. Drag the slider at the bottom of the Timeline to zoom out. Once you see the entire project, you can think about trimming it.

FIGURE 5.14 The Timeline so far, showing the zoomed-out view to see the entire song.

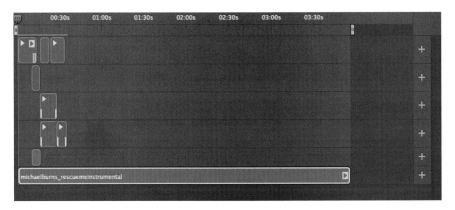

4. Grab the end of the music track and drag all the way to left until the length of the music track is the same as the rest of the project as shown in **FIGURE 5.15**. It will snap into place.

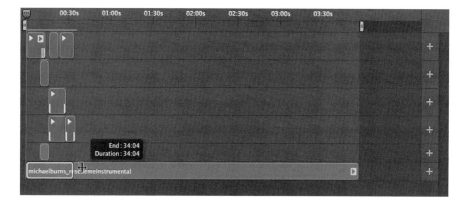

FIGURE 5.15 Trimming the music to fit the rest of the project.

TIP Typically, most modern music naturally builds over time, picking up intensity and more instruments as it goes. This is a way that musicians keep the song interesting to the listeners. Because a lot of video projects are shorter in length, the music never has a chance to build. In this case, trim the beginning of the track so the music starts in a more intense portion of the song.

5. The music is competing with the vocal track right now, so it needs to be adjusted to add flavor but not take over the sound. Ctrl-click/right-click the audio track to make some changes. Drop the Volume down to about 9%. It should mix nicely with the spoken narration now. If you don't like the mix, keep playing with it.

6. Set the Fade Out to 2 seconds, as shown in **FIGURE 5.16**, so that everything ends gracefully. There is no need to set the fade for the beginning of the audio track because the music is starting from the beginning of the song.

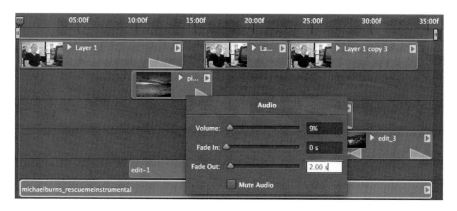

FIGURE 5.16 Making adjustments to the audio settings of the music track.

Mixing the Audio

When the main speech and music are mixed, it's time to finesse the audio. At this point, listen to the audio carefully. Do some of the sounds feel too loud? Too soft? What is the most important thing on the project? In this case, the narration is the main audio component, because it's telling the story. Make sure that everything else *supports* the story you are telling. No one cares how cool a sound is or how difficult it was to capture. What people care about is the message you are communicating. Nothing should be bringing attention to itself. All the parts should be a symphony of the whole. To tweak the audio slightly, follow these steps:

1. At about 22 seconds, the sound of the waves crashing on the beach is a little loud and causes a distraction. To drop the volume on that clip a little bit, first select that clip on Layer 1 in the Timeline. Ctrl-click/right-click and select the music note as shown in FIGURE 5.17.

FIGURE 5.17 The audio options on a video track on the Timeline.

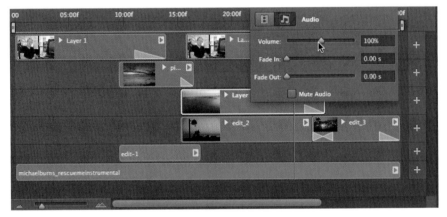

FIGURE 5.18 Changing the Volume to 80%.

2. Reduce the Volume to 80% as shown in FIGURE 5.18, and play it through to make sure that everything sounds balanced. At this point, you should be happy with the project's audio.

There is a reason to work on the audio before finalizing the color and editing the video. The audio serves as a base for the editing, and you will set the timing of the clips and effects to the beat of the music. A good editor will find the beat and rhythm in every video project. You, too, will find it with practice. The next chapter explores color and filters for bringing the project to life visually.

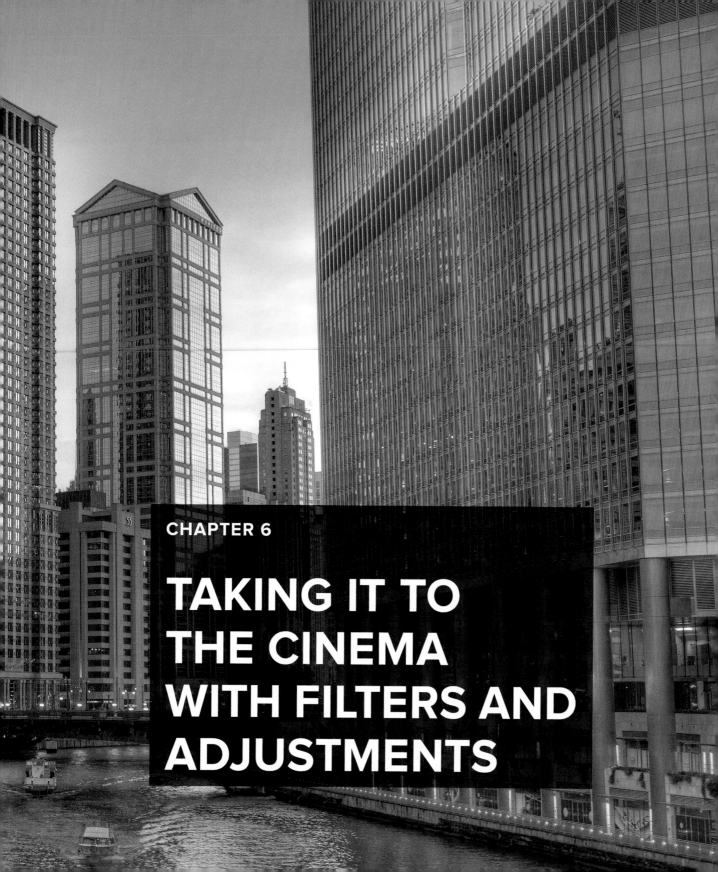

CHAPTER 6

TAKING IT TO THE CINEMA WITH FILTERS AND ADJUSTMENTS

HAVE YOU EVER WATCHED a movie's deleted scenes and been shocked by how different they look from the scenes included in the final release? What is it that makes those final scenes look so cinematic? One noteworthy thing is the coloring treatment that takes your footage from an ordinary-looking video to a stunning cinematic look.

It's one thing to cut some footage. It's an entirely different thing to add eye-popping effects with adjustments and filters. In this chapter, you learn how to make video look better by fixing tone and color problems. Then, fasten your seatbelt because you are about to make your video look ready for the big screen!

Altering an Image with Adjustments

Image adjustments, which are sometimes wrongly referred to as filters, offer ways to change the color and tone. Despite the term "image," image adjustments are not limited to static images—they also work nicely on video. Use this toolset to alter the color and brighten or darken videos. Although the image adjustment features are practical in nature, they can also be used to create a variety of eye-popping effects. You can find all these options under Image > Adjustments as shown in **FIGURE 6.1**.

To use image adjustments, you can't just apply one to a video directly. If you do, you will be in for a nasty surprise as the adjustment will affect only a single frame of video. This is easy to fix by either using adjustment layers or converting the video to a Smart Object, both of which are covered in this chapter.

FIGURE 6.1 The adjustments available in the Image menu.

Using Adjustment Layers

Adjustment layers are exactly the same as adjustments, but they affect an entire layer or multiple layers. They are completely nondestructive, which means they don't damage any pixels and can be changed at any time—even after a document has been closed and reopened. But, most important of all in this scenario, they work perfectly on a video clip on the Timeline. **FIGURE 6.2** shows where to access the adjustment layers in the Layers panel.

Advantages of adjustment layers include:

- Nondestructive

- Re-editable

- Many can be stacked together

- The stacking order can be changed

- Control over which layers are affected

- Opacity adjustments to control the strength of filters

- Blend modes for each adjustment to produce nice effects

- Each comes with a mask, so you can control where it affects the video

- Adjustment layer masks can be animated

Many image adjustment are available in Photoshop, and it's beyond the scope of this book to go through each and every one. The two essential adjustments are covered here: Levels and Curves.

FIGURE 6.2 Adjustment layers are the best way to go for color correcting video.

TIP Learn all about levels and how to use them to adjust your images and video. You'll find a video tutorial named **levels.mp4** in your downloads. This is from the PhotoshopCAFE video, *Photoshop CS6 for Digital Photographers*.

Working with Levels

The Levels adjustment provides an easy way to increase lightness, increase darkness, or adjust the midtones of an image or video as shown in **FIGURE 6.3**. Notice the three triangles under the histogram:

- **Black Point Input Slider (Shadows):** The left triangle is the Black Point Input slider, which sets the black point. Sliding this to the right darkens the shadows. All pixels to the left of the slider turn black.

- **White Point Input Slider (Highlights):** The right triangle is the White Point Input slider, which sets the white point. Moving this slider to the left lightens the highlights. The pixels turn solidly white above this slider, and no pixels display to the right of it. They will be clipped (turned solidly white).

- **Midtones:** The center slider controls the midtones. Slide it to the left to brighten the grays, and slide it to the right to darken the grays.

FIGURE 6.3 An image before and after the Levels are adjusted.

Working with Curves

TIP Because adjusting Curves is really worth learning, you'll find a video tutorial named **curves.mp4** included in your download of files for this book. This video is from the video *Photoshop CS6 For Digital Photographers*, available from photoshopCAFE.com.

Of all the correction tools available, adjusting Curves offers the most possible precision. Curves can target any tone in the image and increase or reduce it, and you have exact control over the entire image. **FIGURE 6.4** shows the same image before and after adjusting Curves.

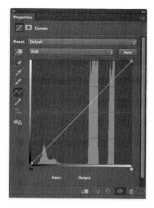

FIGURE 6.4 Before and after Curves adjustment. Notice that Curves allow you to target a specific tone in the video.

To adjust Curves, click on the actual curve to add a point. Drag up to brighten or down to darken the selected range of tones. To the left are shadows and to the right are highlights.

Curves can also be used for color correction. Click RGB and choose one of the color channels to adjust as shown in **FIGURE 6.5**. At this point, adjust it the same as a regular curve, but you are adjusting one color channel at a time.

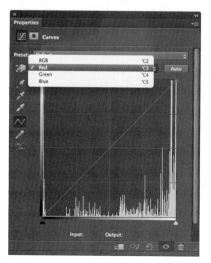

FIGURE 6.5 Choosing an individual color channel in Curves.

Colorizing with Adjustment Layers

TIP If for any reason, you receive a "Cannot locate missing media" warning, read the "Saving and Managing Projects" section in Chapter 3 to learn about relinking files.

To make the video look more professional, it's time to adjust the color and tone using a few different techniques. While experimenting with these techniques, you will look at different ways to work with adjustment layers.

Applying an Adjustment Layer

In this example, you will apply a Vibrance adjustment layer to boost the colors in the sunset.

1. Open the file **ch6-start.psd** from the **ch6** folder, which you will use for the following exercises. Scrub through the Timeline until the ocean and the basketball players are visible as shown in **FIGURE 6.6**. The color of the sky is coming from the basketball footage. Click on the clip to select it.

FIGURE 6.6 Choose the basketball clip in the Timeline.

2. Click on the circle at the bottom of the Layers panel to choose an adjustment layer. Select Vibrance from the list. In the Properties Inspector, drag the Vibrance slider to 73 as shown in **FIGURE 6.7**. This boosts the orange colors in the clip and adds some visual punch to the video.

TIP An adjustment layer affects all the layers underneath it. Therefore, to affect only the basketball clip, you would create the adjustment layer directly above the clip in the layer stack. To affect the entire project, you would click the top layer, so the new adjustment layer is positioned on top of the layer stack.

Using a LUT

LUTs are "lookup tables," which are used in film color grading. LUTs use a table of data to replace the colors on an image to simulate how a film appears when projected. In layperson's terms, you can use these adjustments to simulate different types of cinematic looks. Technically, Photoshop uses a CLUT, or a "color lookup table," and it's found under the Color Lookup option in the Adjustment Layer menu. Follow these steps to see how it works:

1. At the beginning of the working project, notice the handsome model speaking. (It's actually me. I would have much preferred to have used someone else, but I was available and willing to work cheap.) Select the clip by clicking on it in the Timeline.

2. We need to find a good frame to look at while making the adjustment. Scrub through the video until you reach a frame that shows the typical color as a visual reference point. (In this case, the color is all pretty much the same throughout the entire clip.) FIGURE 6.8 shows the project loaded up in Photoshop.

3. To add a Hollywood-style look to the video, first click the circle at the bottom of the Layers panel to open the Adjustment Layers menu. Choose Color Lookup from the list.

4. When you see the options, click on the Abstract menu to the right of the radial button. Choose the Gold-Blue option from the list that appears. You will see that a cinematic look has been applied to the footage (FIGURE 6.9).

FIGURE 6.8 Choosing a frame to prepare to work on the color.

FIGURE 6.9 A Color Look applied to the footage.

Adding a Mask

This Hollywood style looks great on the footage, but it's not too flattering on the skin-tones. The solution is to apply a mask. That's right, a layer mask will work with video! See the "Layer Masks" sidebar for more about masks.

1. Every adjustment layer comes with its very own layer mask. Click the white mask to the right of the Color Lookup adjustment layer.

2. Select the Brush tool in the Tools panel, and then select a soft-edged brush. Make sure the foreground color is set to black in the color swatches on the Tools panel.

3. Paint over the skintones in the video. You will see the original color come back as you mask out the areas. **FIGURE 6.10** shows the footage with the LUT applied to everything except the portions that are masked out.

FIGURE 6.10 A mask applied to the adjustment layer.

4. The change is too noticeable, so the skintones need to be toned back a little to look more natural. With the mask selected, select Window > Properties to open the Properties panel. Change the density to 71% and notice that it fades out the masked area (**FIGURE 6.11**). This gives a much more natural, less overbearing look to the mask.

FIGURE 6.11 Changing the density of the layer mask to produce a more pleasing and natural look to the skintones.

LAYER MASKS

A layer mask is a great way to control the visibility of a portion of a mask. (If you try to use the Eraser tool for this purpose, it will delete the contents of the layer wherever it's used.) Instead of using the Eraser tool, you can paint on a mask with a black brush and hide the corresponding area of the layer. To bring back the visibility, paint the area white. Shades of gray will erase the portion of the mask at varying degrees of opacity: 50% gray is 50% transparent, 25% gray is 25% opaque. The amount of transparency is directly proportional to the amount of black on the mask. For video purposes, masks are very useful.

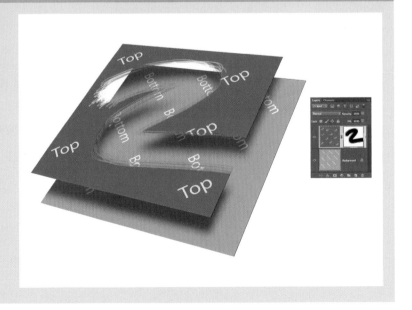

Animating Masks on Adjustments

For many purposes, the mask would be perfect on the footage and would most certainly be sufficient for a still image. The problem is, I am moving my head around as I'm speaking. This is causing the head to move in and out of the mask and revealing colored edges.

The solution is to make the mask move with the head. To do that, first isolate the area where there is movement and see how bad it is. Though not necessary, I find it useful to create guides to show the area of movement. This helps in planning and working with the mask.

1. Press Command+R (Ctrl+R) to display rulers across the top and down the left side of the window. Select the Move tool and drag a guide from the top ruler and release it at the top of the head. Drag out a guide from the side and drop it to the right of my head as shown in **FIGURE 6.12**. You can move the guides at any time by dragging them with the Move tool.

2. Scrub through the video until the head moves to the left side. Drag out a third guide and drop it on the left edge as shown in **FIGURE 6.13**.

FIGURE 6.12 Setting guides on the top and right side.

FIGURE 6.13 Boxing in the area of movement with guides.

3. Keep scrubbing through the video clip. If any part of the head moves outside the guides, move the guide out to compensate. When you are done, all the movement should be contained inside the guides (**FIGURES 6.14** and **6.15**).

FIGURES 6.14 and **6.15** The guides define the area where movement is happening in the object being masked.

Working with comments

Now that the area of movement is defined, you need to know the timing. When working in Adobe Premiere Pro, I would use Timeline markers, but Photoshop doesn't have Timeline markers. Instead, you can use Photoshop's Timeline comments, which are great for collaboration and reminders as well. To use Timeline comments as markers, mark the points where the head moves back and forth.

1. First, enable the Timeline comments. Click the small triangle at the top-right corner of the Timeline to display the panel options and select Show > Comments Track (**FIGURE 6.16**). At the very top of the tracks on the Timeline, you will now see a Comments strip. It will say Comments on the left column and have a stopwatch icon.

FIGURE 6.16 Turning on Timeline comments.

2. Scrub the playhead until the head in the video moves to one side and stop there. To add a marker, click the stopwatch by the Comment track. When the Edit Timeline Comment dialog displays, type the single letter l (a lowercase L, for *left*) into the field (**FIGURE 6.17**) and click OK.

FIGURE 6.17 Adding a Timeline comment.

3. A small box is added above the Timeline to indicate a comment. Scrub forward until the next head movement. Notice that a diamond displays to the left of the stop-watch. Click the diamond from now on to add markers. Keep scrubbing and adding markers each time the head flips over to the other side. When you are finished, the Timeline should look like the one shown in **FIGURE 6.18**, with several markers on it.

FIGURE 6.18 Markers indicating where the movement happens on the Timeline.

FIGURE 6.19 The mask back at 100% density and cleaned up around the edges.

Animating masks

The new markers on the Timeline indicate when the movement happens and guides indicate where it happens. It's time to animate the mask to follow the movement. With the groundwork done with the guides and markers, it's quite easy to do the rest. To prepare to move the mask, follow these steps:

1. Select the mask on the Color Lookup adjustment layer. Change the mask's Density to 100% in the Properties panel as shown in **FIGURE 6.19**. This will make it easier to see what the mask is affecting. If you need to, use the Brush tool (set to black or white) and make the mask more accurate by tightening up any overflow.

2. The last thing to do before animating the mask is to drag the adjustment layer to the very top of the layer stack. Make sure the layer isn't in a layer group, but by itself at the top as shown in **FIGURE 6.20**. If it's in a layer group, you won't have access to all the keyframes. Also, make sure the duration is the same as the video clip. Drag the ends of the adjustment layer to change its duration, just as you do with a video or graphics clip.

3. Now, to move the mask with the movement of the talking head, click the triangle to the left of Color Lookup 1 on the Timeline. This opens the keyframe options. With the playhead on frame 1, click the stopwatch to the left of the Layer Mask Position. This adds the first keyframe (**FIGURE 6.21**) so you can animate the Layer Mask Position.

FIGURE 6.20 The adjustment layer at the top of the layer stack.

FIGURE 6.21 Adding the first keyframe for the Layer Mask Position.

4. Scrub the video to the first comment marker, which indicates the end of a head movement. Make sure the layer mask is still selected in the Layers panel. With the Move tool, drag the mask over so it covers the head of the speaker (FIGURE 6.22). Notice that an additional keyframe is created automatically.

FIGURE 6.22 Moving the mask with the head.

5. Continue moving the playhead to each comment marker and moving the mask to match. A new keyframe will be added each time. Play it through a couple of times, looking for areas that the mask doesn't move quite in time with the head. If it looks off, just move the mask with the Move tool and the keyframe will be added. It's actually quite easy to do this and much quicker than it may seem. **FIGURES 6.23** and **6.24** show the keyframes added along with a couple more after a little bit of tweaking. The mask is nicely animated with the head and it's hard to tell a mask is even there now.

FIGURE 6.23 Animating the mask with the movement in the video.

FIGURE 6.24 Tweaking the animation.

6. Now that the mask is moving correctly, the color is only masked out on the skin-tones. To make it look natural again, lower the mask's Density a little to around 56% as shown in **FIGURE 6.25**. Use a value that looks good to you.

FIGURE 6.25 Lowering the mask's Density to 56%.

TIP Remember, you can use this mask technique for a number of different things, including motion graphics. A mask is a mask. Be creative.

Using effect and layer controls

Let's split hairs for a moment. When you see the video fading into the photographic slide of the misty water, the effect isn't working on only the talking head layer—it's affecting all the layers underneath it. This is evident by the fact that the adjustment layer isn't fading out with the video clip; it just runs out at the end of it (**FIGURE 6.26**).

Adding a transition isn't the answer because it won't fade out correctly with the video. You need to find a way for the color adjustment to affect only the video layer with the talking head in it. You can easily achieve this with a clipping group, which will cause an adjustment layer to affect only the layer or the video layer directly under it.

In the Layers panel, position the pointer on the line between the adjustment layer and the layer group. When an arrow displays as shown in **FIGURE 6.27**, Option-click/Alt-click to clip the adjustment to the video clip (or video group) directly under it. This will give you the ability to adjust just the one layer (the talking head), as seen in **FIGURE 6.28**.

FIGURE 6.26 Before the adjustment is clipped to the video group.

FIGURE 6.27 The icon to indicate clipping the adjustment layer.

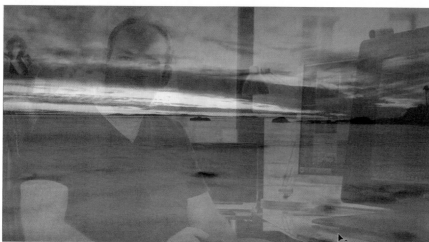

FIGURE 6.28 After the adjustment is clipped to the video group as compared to Figure 6.26.

Converting the Video to Black and White

Who doesn't love the romantic and nostalgic look of black-and-white film? At one time, it was difficult to make a color video look good in black and white. Now, it's such a cinch that you can do it while sipping on your morning coffee or Earl Grey, if you please.

1. With the top layer selected in the Layers panel, click the Adjustment Layer button. Select Black & White from the options. The entire video turns black and white in a single click as shown in **FIGURE 6.29**. Go ahead, preview the video.

FIGURE 6.29 Adding a Black & White adjustment.

2. Trim the beginning of the adjustment to come in at the same time as the basketball players and the water on the beach as shown in **FIGURE 6.30**. Notice how you can affect only the parts of the Timeline that the adjustment is placed over. You can control both layers and time, too.

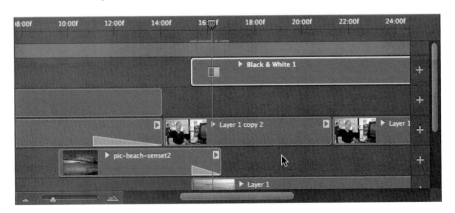

FIGURE 6.30 Trimming the adjustment layer.

3. Drag the Black & White adjustment layer down in the Layers panel to reposition it as shown in **FIGURE 6.31**. Place it on top of the video group that contains the basketball clip. You will notice that only the basketball clip is now in black and white.

FIGURE 6.31 Applying the Black & White adjustment to the basketball clip only.

Fading an Adjustment Over Time

Now that the Black & White adjustment is applied, you will fade it out over time to reveal the beautiful orange sunset on the basketball clip.

1. Move the playhead about 4 seconds into the Black & White adjustment (frame 20). This should give the audience enough time to enjoy the black-and-white effect.

2. If the keyframe options are not open, click the triangle next to the Black & White track. Click the stopwatch on Opacity to set the first keyframe. **FIGURE 6.32** shows the keyframe.

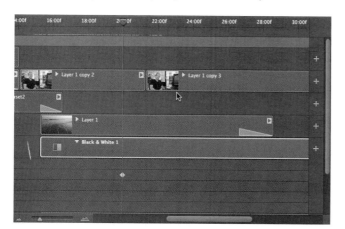

FIGURE 6.32 Setting the initial keyframe on the Black & White layer.

3. Advance the playhead 1 second to prepare to make a quick transition from Black & White into color.

4. In the Black & White layer in the Layers panel, reduce the Opacity to 0. This essentially hides the adjustment and allows the color to show through (**FIGURE 6.33**). The new keyframe is automatically added. Preview the video to see the effect in action.

FIGURE 6.33 Fading out the Black & White effect.

Save your file as Ch6-end.psd. To compare your results to mine, view **ch6-end.psd** in your downloads.

Filters as Adjustment Layers

Photoshop offers a lot of filters and many can be used on video. The key is to first convert the video track into a Smart Object so filters can work as adjustments. To convert footage to a Smart Object, Ctrl-click/right-click the layer name and choose Convert to Smart Object from the context menu (**FIGURE 6.34**).

FIGURE 6.34 Convert your video track into a Smart Object.

Smart Objects for Video

Once the video is a Smart Object, many filters will now work on the entire video layer. It's quite easy to tell which ones work, because they will be the ones that aren't grayed out when the clip is converted to a Smart Object. A Smart Object is actually just a container. When you convert a layer (or multiple layers) to a Smart Object, this is what happens: A container is created and called a Smart Object. Whatever is selected when you create the Smart Object is stuffed into the container (**FIGURE 6.35**).

FIGURE 6.35 The top layer is a Smart Object.

If you want to access the original files, you simply double-click the Smart Object in the Layers panel. The contents of the container (the original content that was built into the Smart Object) then opens inside a new document (**FIGURE 6.36**). I'm going to use this video of a plane for a quick example but you're welcome to look at the basketball video example we've been using to see the options in the Layers panel I'm referring to.

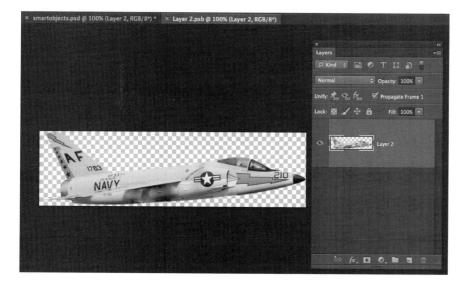

FIGURE 6.36 A new document with the Smart Object contents.

If you make changes, save the document, and close it, the Smart Object will update automatically (**FIGURE 6.37**). The temporary documents are in the .psb format so that they are able to hold large files if needed (**FIGURE 6.38**).

FIGURE 6.37 A modified image.

FIGURE 6.38 An updated Smart Object in the main document.

When you apply filters, they are actually applied to the Smart Object. Because your clips are in this Smart Object container, they are affected. This is brilliant because you now have a way to affect the entire video clip and not just a single frame. When a filter is applied to a Smart Object, it's called a Smart Filter because it can be edited later (**FIGURE 6.39**).

Double-click the filter in the Layers panel to display options such as Blending Mode and Opacity. You can control these properties on a filter-by-filter basis, which gives you the same control you have with an adjustment layer (**FIGURE 6.40**).

Smart Objects also come with masks. These masks can be painted to hide portions of the Smart Filters (**FIGURE 6.41**).

FIGURE 6.39 A motion blur applied as a Smart Filter.

FIGURE 6.40 Modifying a Smart Object.

FIGURE 6.41 Masking a portion of the Smart Filter.

Also, note that you can have multiple Smart Filters applied to a single Smart Object. Now this is smart indeed.

Shadow Highlight as a Smart Filter

The Shadow/Highlight filter is immensely useful for video because it's used to recover detail in the shadows and the highlights without blowing out the rest of the footage. Essentially, this gives the appearance of increasing the dynamic range of the footage. The result is details in shadows and highlights simultaneouly.

There is a catch, though. Notice that this adjustment is missing from the adjustment layers. If you apply it through Image > Adjustments, it will affect only a single frame.

The trick to getting the Shadow/Highlight filter to work on an entire clip is to use a Smart Filter. (Shadow/Highlight is the one adjustment that works on video as a Smart Filter.) The key is to convert the clip to a Smart Object. Here are the steps:

1. Open the video clip **river.m4v** from the **footage** folder in the download.

2. Ctrl-click/right-click the layer name and choose Convert to Smart Object from the menu (**FIGURE 6.42**).

FIGURE 6.42 The river footage converted to a Smart Object.

3. Now that the video track is converted to a Smart Object, you can apply the Shadow/Highlight adjustment as a Smart Filter. Choose Image > Adjustment > Shadow/Highlight.

4. Adjust the Shadows settings as shown in **FIGURE 6.43** and see how much detail shows in the shadows of the video clip in **FIGURE 6.44**.

5. Now, make some changes to the Highlight settings (**FIGURE 6.45**). This is where this adjustment is really beautiful. See how much detail is restored in the highlight regions of the footage (**FIGURE 6.46**).

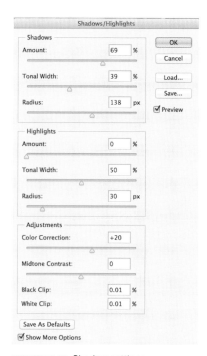

FIGURE 6.43 Shadow settings.

FIGURE 6.44 More detail showing in shadows. Compare this with Figure 6.42.

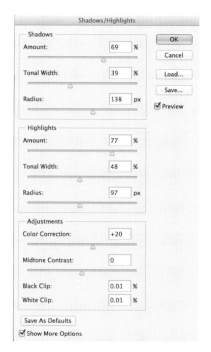

FIGURE 6.45 Settings for the Highlights.

FIGURE 6.46 Much more detail is now recovered in the highlight portions of the footage.

6. Make some tweaks that set the flavor by changing the color correction and the midtone contrast. The final and very important step is to set a Black Clip percentage or the footage will look washed out (**FIGURE 6.47**). The Black Clip adjustment forces the shadow areas to pure black, which adds some body to the footage.

If you want to see the final footage with Shadow/HIghlights, check out the **shad highlight.psd** file in the **ch2** folder. Compare **FIGURE 6.48** with the original. You can see how this adjustment will be your best friend when it comes to restoring highlights, opening up shadows, and otherwise pulling out the detail in your footage.

The project is looking really good now. The next chapter looks at text and motion graphics. This is a lot of fun and it gives the project a professional commercial look.

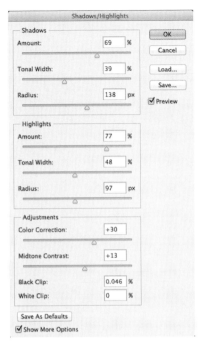

FIGURE 6.47 Final adjustments to Shadow/Highlights.

FIGURE 6.48 The final footage after Shadow/Highlights.

CHAPTER 7

ADDING ANIMATION AND MOTION GRAPHICS

WHEN YOU WATCH DOCUMENTARIES, commercials, and news and sports programs, you see all kinds of spiffy graphics and titles. Animated graphics move across the screen with effortless ease. Perhaps, you're thinking that motion graphics are beyond you and too difficult. Or you may be dying to know the limits, so that you can break them. Either way, this is the chapter that shows how to make things move in Photoshop, and it may be the most fun chapter in the book.

Creating Animations with Keyframes

If you have been following the exercises in the book, you have already used keyframes a little bit. This chapter provides greater detail, explains how they work, and features more things you can do with keyframe animations.

Keyframes are the essential tool used for creating animations. When a keyframe is added, it acts as a "listener" that waits for another keyframe to give it instructions. (Just to be clear, "listener" isn't an official term, it's a term I coined to help explain what is happening.) Once a second keyframe is detected, Photoshop creates an animation between the two keyframes on the Timeline. Once the first keyframe is set, Photoshop uses auto keyframes whenever you change a setting. You will see in the lesson that follows.

This simple example explains keyframes and then you can roll up your sleeves and try it on your project. I warn you! This is fun!

Starting with two layers on a Timeline, you will animate only the top layer of the flying car shown in **FIGURE 7.1**. This exercise clearly illustrates how keyframes work.

1. Open the **flyingcar.psd** file from the **ch7** folder. Click the triangle to the left of the track name to reveal the keyframes. **FIGURE 7.2** shows the typical options for graphics or video keyframes. The controls work as follows:

   ▪ **Position:** Makes it possible to animate an object across the screen.

   ▪ **Opacity:** Allows things to fade in and out from solid to transparency.

   ▪ **Style:** Allows the properties of a layer style to change over time.

2. When beginning to animate any property, click its stopwatch once. This sets the initial keyframe listener. In this example, shown in **FIGURE 7.3**, a keyframe is set on frame 1 for Position. Notice, that the object is moved to its starting position on the layer. You will make it move across the screen.

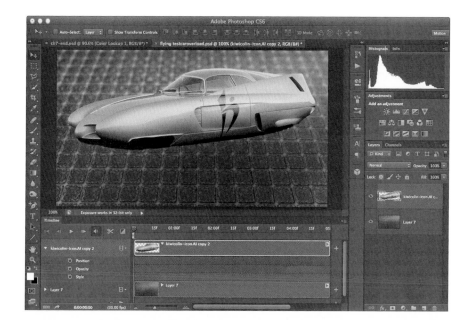

FIGURE 7.1 The starting project.

FIGURE 7.2 Basic keyframes revealed.

FIGURE 7.3 Setting the first keyframe.

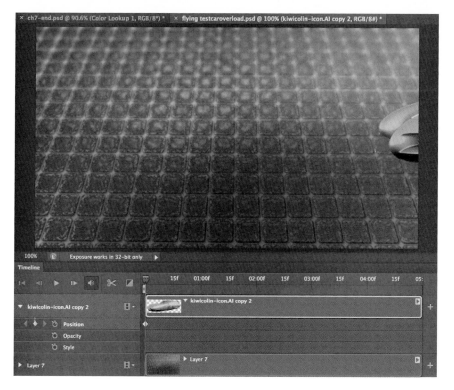

3. Move the playhead to the point in time where you want the animated move to conclude as shown in **FIGURE 7.4**.

FIGURE 7.4 Move the playhead to indicate the end of the animation.

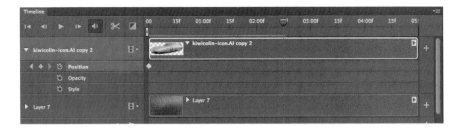

4. Using the Move tool, drag the object to the desired ending position as shown in **FIGURE 7.5**. Notice that a new "auto" keyframe is automatically created; this tells Photoshop that there is a new position and to create an animated "tween" between the two positions.

FIGURE 7.5 Changing the position of the object on the screen adds an animation.

TIP A tween is an animation term that is short for in-between frames. In traditional animation, the lead artists draw the key frames, or key moments of action in an animation. Junior animators then draw all the in-between frames that complete the smooth animation. Photoshop creates all the in-between frames for you in a process known as tweening.

5. Scrub the playhead and you will notice that an animation happens between the two keyframes as shown in **FIGURE 7.6**.

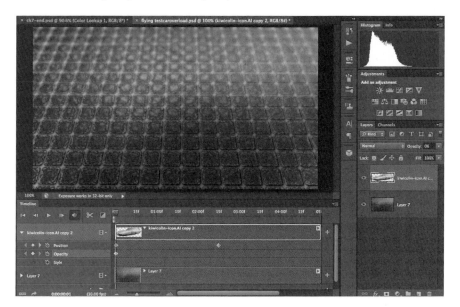

FIGURE 7.6 The animation in action.

To try another animation type, Opacity, follow these steps.

1. Put the playhead at the first frame. Click the stopwatch under Opacity.

2. Reduce the Opacity to 0 on the Layers panel as shown in **FIGURE 7.7**.

FIGURE 7.7 Adding a keyframe for opacity animation.

3. Move the playhead forward in time and change the Opacity to 100% in the Layers panel as shown in **FIGURE 7.8**. When you scrub the Timeline, notice that the object now fades in over time.

FIGURE 7.8 Creating an opacity-fading tween.

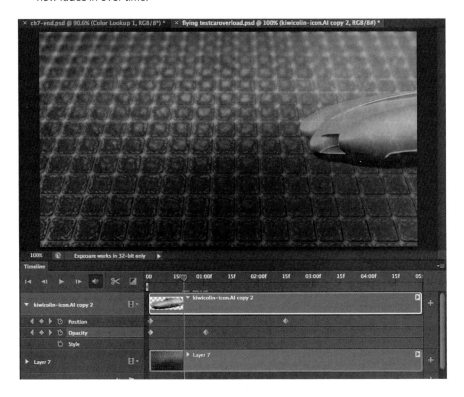

Modifying Keyframes

Once you know how to create keyframes, you can modify them. Once you have set keyframes, you aren't stuck with the timing. It's very easy to change the timing of animations. In fact, animators spend more time finessing the timing of an animation than they do creating them.

Changing the Speed of an Animation

If you look at **FIGURE 7.9**, notice there are 2.5 seconds between the keyframes. This means the animation will last 2.5 seconds.

FIGURE 7.9 Select a keyframe by clicking it. A selected keyframe is yellow.

To move a keyframe, drag its yellow diamond on the Timeline. When a keyframe is changed, for example if the time between the two frames is decreased to 1.5 seconds (**FIGURE 7.10**), what do you think happens to the animation? The object moves the same physical distance in less time, which means the animation will appear faster.

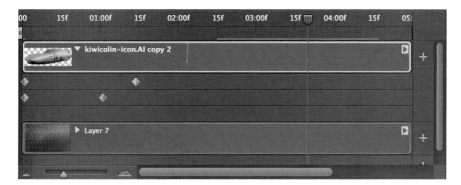

TIP To increase the speed of an animation, move the keyframes closer together. To slow down an animation, move the keyframes further apart.

FIGURE 7.10 Drag to reposition a keyframe in the Timeline.

Retiming an Animation

You can change when an animation happens on the Timeline while maintaining the speed and look. All you need to do is move the keyframes without changing the amount of space between them. You can select and move two or more keyframes.

1. Drag-select or Shift-click to select both keyframes on the Timeline. They should both display in yellow as shown in **FIGURE 7.11**.

2. Drag both keyframes to change when the animation happens on the Timeline as shown in **FIGURE 7.12**.

FIGURE 7.11 Selecting multiple keyframes on the Timeline.

FIGURE 7.12 Moving multiple keyframes together.

EASING

Easing is a way to mimic real-world movement. If you've ever used After Effects or Flash, you may have noticed the lack of easing controls. In the real world, most movement isn't constant—things speed up as they gather momentum and slow down to stop. Think about starting and stopping an elevator or car, or closing a door. This nonconstant movement is called easing. To ease-out is to start slow and then ramp up to full speed. To ease-in is to slowdown the movement near the end and gently bring it to a stop.

At this time, Photoshop has no easing controls, but you can use a little trick to fake it. It's not as good as the real thing, but with some patience, you can use this technique to add more realism to your motion tweens.

Begin with a basic 3-second motion animation. The movement is constant and comes to a screaming halt.

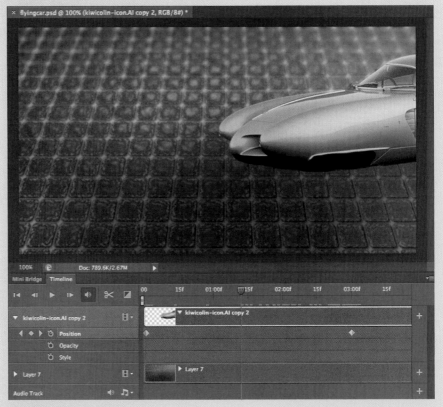

A 3-second motion animation.

Decide where you want the action to begin to slow down. Then, add a keyframe a few more frames to the right. Move the playhead and click the diamond icon by the stopwatch to add a keyframe. The motion is split into two parts, but the timing doesn't change, so there's no change in movement yet.

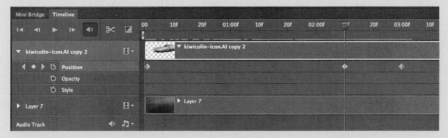

Adding an intermediate keyframe.

Drag the keyframe to the left. You have taken that split motion and changed the duration of both sides. By dragging to the left, it shortens the amount of frames on the left of the keyframe for the same movement, thus slightly speeding up the movement. On the right, by adding more frames between the movement, you have now slowed down the motion. Go ahead and test it, and you'll see where it slows down.

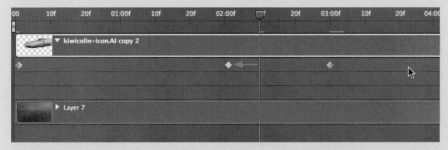

Changing the timing of the keyframe by dragging to the left.

Add another intermediate keyframe to further split the timing near the end.

Move the keyframe to the left to slow down the movement near the end. This adds an extra step of easing. It may take some practice and experimentation to get this technique down pat. But it is a useful tool when you need it.

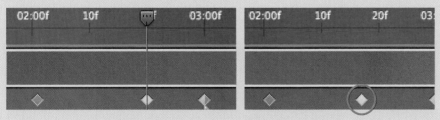

Adding a second intermediate keyframe.   Two easing steps are better than one.

FIGURE 7.13 Creating a blank layer for the title bar.

✓ **TIP** Watch the video from PhotoshopCAFE (**motion_graphics.mp4**) that teaches you how to create a lower third graphic from scratch and animate it.

✓ **TIP** You can also use the Rectangular Marquee tool or one of the shape tools. Just make sure the options are set to pixels for the shape tools.

Lower Thirds

A "lower third" is a graphic placed in the lower portion of the screen. Often, it's an animated bar used for titling. It's the sort of thing you see all the time on TV when you're watching sports or news programs. Lower thirds are really quite easy to make and they can add significant polish to your video presentations.

1. If your file is open from the previous chapter, you can use that in these steps. Or, open **ch7-start.psd** from the **ch7** folder. Make sure the playhead is at the beginning of the Timeline.

Creating a Lower Third Graphic

2. Create a new layer at the top of the Layers panel and name it "title bar" as shown in **FIGURE 7.13**.

   You can import a graphic for a title bar or make your own; both methods are shown here.

3. To make a simple title bar, select the Polygonal Lasso tool. This is a great tool for creating the kinds of shapes used for lower thirds.

   The Polygonal Lasso tool works similar to polygon tools in page layout applications and other programs. Each mouse click defines a section of straight line. The first click creates an anchor point, and when you move the mouse, you see a line follow it like an anchored piece of thread. When you click again, it anchors the point and then you continue to drag the thread. When you are ready to close the loop, click on the start point or press Return/Enter on the keyboard. You will see a "marching ants" selection or marquee. Don't worry—it's easier than it sounds.

   The key to getting a good shape for a rectangular graphic is holding down the Shift key to constrain the angles to 45-degree increments. Create a selection similar to **FIGURE 7.14** with the Polygonal Lasso tool.

FIGURE 7.14 Making a selection with the Polygonal Lasso tool.

4. Fill the shape with a gradient or a solid color as shown in **FIGURE 7.15**. Press Cmd+D/Ctrl+D to turn off the selection. We have finished filling the shape, so we no longer need a selection.

FIGURE 7.15 Filling the title bar with a colored gradient.

Importing Graphics to Use as Animations

The lower third you just created will serve its purpose here. However, you can try something fancier with an imported graphic such as the one I created with the Polygonal Lasso tool. This graphic is dressed up a bit with text and shapes.

1. To bring the graphic into the project, open the **pixeloverload.psd** file from the **ch7** folder in your download. Select both of its layers and drag them to the title bar of the working document as shown in **FIGURE 7.16**.

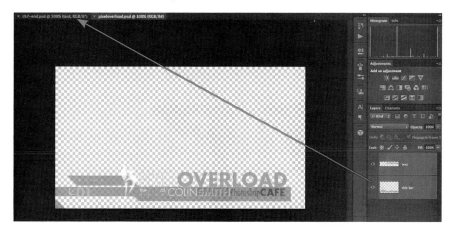

FIGURE 7.16 Transferring the graphic from one document to another in Photoshop.

2. When you release the mouse button, the project window comes to the front and the graphic is dropped into the document. Drag the clips to the beginning of the Timeline if necessary and position the graphic onscreen where you want it. (**FIGURE 7.17** shows the graphics in the project.)

   You can also use File > Place to bring logos and other pre-existing graphics into the project.

FIGURE 7.17 The lower third graphic positioned on the video.

Adding the Title Text

At this point, you will add the title text. Select the Type tool, click in the document, and start typing. This creates a new layer that you can use for entering and formatting text. Alternatively, you can use the rasterized type from the imported graphic. The layer is called **text**.

You will use two animations on the lower third: The first will fade-in the text and the second will animate the bar and the text that slides into the screen.

1. Add some new text or use the text in the imported graphic. Your document should have two layers as shown in **FIGURE 7.18**: "title bar" and "text.: Select the text layer to fade it in from transparency.

FIGURE 7.18 Lower third title bar and text.

2. In Frame 1, click the stopwatch to turn on the Opacity keyframes as shown in **FIGURE 7.19**. Change the Opacity to 0 in the Layers panel. The text should disappear.

FIGURE 7.19 Creating an opacity keyframe animation.

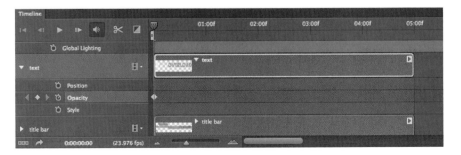

3. Move the playhead forward to 1.5 seconds and increase the Opacity to 100% in the Layers panel. A keyframe will be added with a fade-in of the title text over 1.5 seconds as shown in **FIGURE 7.20**.

FIGURE 7.20 The fade-in animation on the text layer.

Creating a Nested Animation

The next thing to do is slide in both the text layer and the title bar at the same time. You could animate them separately and try to get them exactly the same, but an easier way is to group them together and move both layers as a single object.

If you have experience with Adobe Flash or After Effects, you are probably familiar with the terms "nested animation" or "precomp." Actually, it was my experience working with Flash that gave me the idea for the following workflow.

1. Select the two layers to animate together as shown in **FIGURE 7.21**.

2. Ctrl-click/right-click one of the layer names and choose Convert to Smart Object from the context menu. (See Chapter 6 for a refresher on Smart Objects.)

FIGURE 7.21 Shift-click to select two layers and then select Convert to Smart Object from the context menu.

Both layers are now encapsulated into a single Smart Object as shown in **FIGURE 7.22**. You can see the Smart Object icon in the Layers panel. This Smart Object can now be animated as a single unit.

FIGURE 7.22 The two layers converted to a Smart Object.

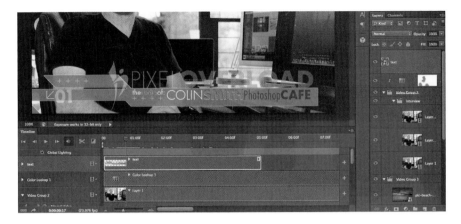

WORKING WITH NESTED SMART OBJECT ANIMATIONS

To work with a single layer in a Smart Object, double-click the Smart Object. It will open as a new document in Photoshop with the objects on their own Timeline as shown in **FIGURE 7.23**. You can make changes to the animations of the individual layers and even add more layers if you like. When you are finished modifying the contents of the Smart Object, close the Smart Object document and click Yes to save the changes. The Smart Object will update in the host document (the main project you're working on).

FIGURE 7.23 The contents of a Smart Object open as a .psb in a separate window.

3. To animate the Smart Object for the lower third, click the Transform Keyframe stopwatch in frame 1. Hold down the Shift key to constrain the movement and slide the lower third graphic off the screen to the left as shown in FIGURE 7.24.

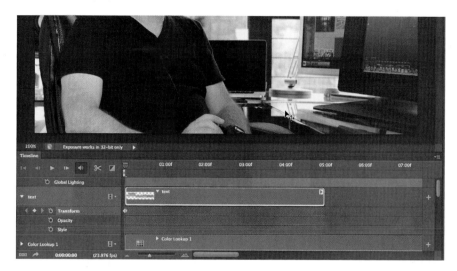

FIGURE 7.24 Creating a new Transform Keyframe animation.

4. Move the playhead to 1.5 seconds. Using the Move tool, Shift-drag the graphic to its end position to create a Transform Keyframe animation. Notice the text and bar slide together while the text is fading in.

FIGURE 7.25 The Transform Keyframe animation.

5. Drop a 1 second fade transition at the end of the lower third as shown in **FIGURE 7.26**. This will cause it to fade out smoothly.

FIGURE 7.26 Add a transition to fade out the lower third.

Creating an Animated Credit Roll

A great way to finish off a project is with an animated credit roll, which scrolls the names of everyone who worked on a project up the screen. Credit rolls are very common at the ends of programs.

This animation requires two parts: the text moving up the screen and a short fade in/ fade out. It's best to do the fades last, because it's very hard to position type on the screen when it's transparent. Also, it's worth mentioning that the fades at the beginning and end can be easily handled with transitions. This lesson illustrates different ways of adding keyframes.

TIP You can create text layers by clicking in the document with the Type tool or clicking in a blank layer. You will then need to change the layer's name.

1. At the top of the Layers panel, create a new layer and name it "credits" as shown in **FIGURE 7.27**.

FIGURE 7.27 The new layer all set for the credits.

2. Using the Type tool, click and drag to create a rectangle as shown in **FIGURE 7.28**. Hold down the Spacebar to reposition the text area as you create it.

FIGURE 7.28 Dragging the Type tool to create paragraph text.

3. Type in the names and titles for your credits. Choose a font, size, color, and alignment such as Arial Bold, 19 point, white, centered.

FIGURE 7.29 Entering some placeholder credit text.

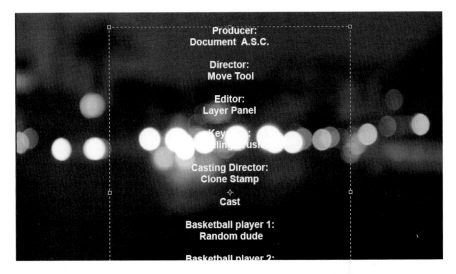

4. Move the credits clip to the end of the project on the Timeline. Move the playhead to the start of the clip.

5. Move the credit text in the document window so only the top line is showing at the bottom of the window as shown in **FIGURE 7.30**.

FIGURE 7.30 Positioning the credit clip on the Timeline.

6. On frame 1 of the credits clip, create a keyframe on the Transform property as shown in FIGURE 7.31. Move the playhead to the end of the track.

FIGURE 7.31 Setting up a Transform Keyframe animation.

7. Drag the text up in the window until only the bottom line of the credit text is showing at the top of the window as shown in FIGURE 7.32. Hold down the Shift key as you drag to constrain the movement to vertical. The text should now scroll up when you test the playback. Drag the edge of the purple clip to change the scroll speed.

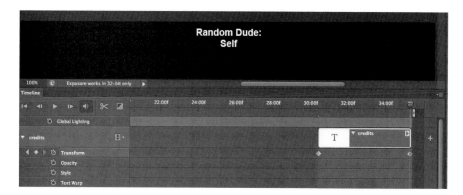

FIGURE 7.32 The end of the animation for the credits.

8. Create the fade effect, starting with fade in. Put the playhead at the beginning of the credits clip. Click a keyframe for Opacity and reduce it to 0 in the Layers panel.

9. Move the playhead forward 1 second. Change the Opacity to 100% and an auto keyframe is added (FIGURE 7.33).

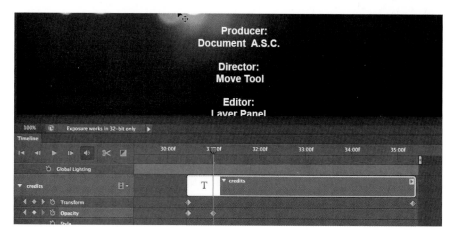

FIGURE 7.33 Fading in the credit roll.

10. Move the playhead to 1 second from the end of the clip as shown in **FIGURE 7.34**. Because the Opacity is remaining at 100% and constant, we can't get an auto keyframe by changing a setting. You must force a keyframe by clicking the diamond between the 3 triangles to the left of the track name in the Timeline.

A keyframe will then appear.

Don't be tempted to click the stopwatch again as many users before you have. All that does is delete all the keyframes on the track and you are back to square one.

FIGURE 7.34 Forcing a keyframe into the Timeline.

11. Finally, move the playhead to the end of the Timeline and reduce the Opacity to 0 in the Layers panel.

12. Now, preview the credit roll and make any adjustments necessary (**FIGURE 7.35**).

FIGURE 7.35 Testing the credit roll.

At this point, the project is actually finished. You can compare your results with the **ch7-end.psd** file in the **ch7** folder. Test the video and when you're happy with it, move to the last chapter and learn how to render the video and show it to the world.

Time-lapse Photography

Time-lapse photography is really enjoying a comeback right now. You can see it on all kinds of commercials, TV shows, and movies—it's when things are moving very fast on the video. The sky zooms by, people and cars move at super speed, and night falls in seconds.

The process involves using a still camera to take photographs at intervals. The images are then displayed at standard 24 or 30fps video to show time progressing very quickly.

Shooting Time-lapse

When shooting time-lapse, you need:

- A camera capable of manual exposure
- A tripod
- Intervalometer or laptop and camera software
- Tripod

I mentioned the need for a tripod twice on purpose. When shooting time-lapse, even the slightest unexpected movement will ruin the series. To capture time-lapse:

1. Set the camera on a tripod and focus and frame the shot.

2. Using manual exposure, set the exposure. It's a good idea to slightly drag the shutter to allow some motion blur into the images. 1/50 of a second or slower should suffice.

3. Using an intervalometer, set the camera to take a certain number of shots at a set interval. For the sequence used here, I set the camera to take 300 photographs at 10 second increments. That means when it's played back at 24 fps, I get 240 seconds worth of activity for every second played back.

Creating Time-lapse Video in Photoshop

Once all of the photographs are captured, its easy to convert them to an image sequence in Photoshop.

1. Choose File > Open and navigate to the folder where you stored your individual images or use the images provided in the **ch4/timelapse** folder.

TIP Some cameras, such as many Nikons, have built-in intervalometers. If you don't have an intervalometer, you might be able to use your camera's software (Canon software, for example, makes it easy). Attach a camera to the laptop to use it. In a jam, I have been known to tap my foot, count down, and press the remote shutter release each time, but I don't recommend this method unless it's an emergency (I was 10,000 feet up a mountain in Maui and my intervalometer broke).

2. In the Open dialog, select the first image in the sequence and check Image Sequence at the bottom as shown in **FIGURE 7.36**.

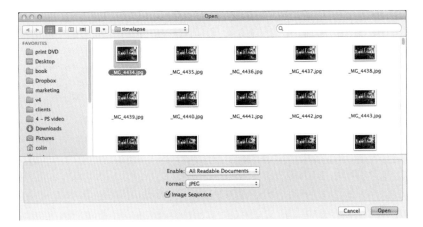

3. In the Frame Rate dialog, choose 24 frames per second and click OK as shown in **FIGURE 7.37**.

   All of the images in the folder are loaded into an image sequence and treated as a video clip as shown in **FIGURE 7.38**.

FIGURE 7.37 Setting the frame rate for the time-lapse sequence.

4. Play it back and enjoy the time-lapse video.

FIGURE 7.38 Viewing the time-lapse as a video in Photoshop.

Using the Tilt-shift Time-lapse Effect

A big trend in photography and video today is the tilt-shift effect. This effect is achieved by blurring all of the image/video except for a strip of sharp focus. This simulates using a tilt-shift lens and produces a minimized effect. This effect works by simulating the blurs used in macro photography.

Until now, creating this with video or an image sequence in Photoshop was very laborious. If you are an Adobe Creative Cloud subscriber, the latest Photoshop update allows the use of the Blur Gallery with a Smart Object. This means that video can now be affected by these blurs, which is wonderful news.

Taking the finished time-lapse from the previous section, add these steps as an alternative.

1. Select the Time-lapse video in the Layers panel. Ctrl-click/right-click and choose Convert to Smart Object from the context menu. The video will now become a Smart Object.

2. From the main menu, choose Filter > Blur > Tilt-Shift. Drag on the lines to move the focus area lower as you see in **FIGURE 7.39**. Apply the settings from Figure 7.39 as well.

FIGURE 7.39 The Settings for the Tilt-Shift blur.

3. Click OK and then preview the miniaturized looking time-lapse sequence as shown in **FIGURE 7.40**. There you go, the latest and greatest.

FIGURE 7.40 The tilt-shift minia-turized looking time-lapse video.

Animating a Layer Styles

Another keyframe option is Style, which you can use to animate different layer style properties. Following is an old trick I do in Flash, which makes the object look very 3D. In fact, you could call it a hyper-real faux 3D shadow.

This is a great effect that you can use time and again. If you really study how things look and behave in the real world, it will enable you to figure out unparalleled realism. I have devoted a great deal of time in my life to looking at things and questioning why things look a certain way or react to light in a certain way. It's called learning how to see, and many other artists I know do the same thing.

If you look at an object moving towards a surface, the defining quality is the shadow. At a distance, it appears soft and transparent. As the object moves closer to another object, the shadow becomes more opaque and harder edged. This simple example simulates this technique, and you will see the amount of realism achieved without deal-ing with expensive 3D rendering of shadows.

Starting with the flying car and a background, two layers in total, you will make it look like the car is hovering and landing.

1. Open the file **flyingcar.psd** from the **ch4** folder in your downloads (**FIGURE 7.41**).

FIGURE 7.41 Open the soon-to-be-hovering car in Photoshop.

2. You will use a layer style to apply a drop shadow to the car object. In the Layers panel, select the car layer, click the little F at the bottom of the Layers panel, and choose Drop Shadow. Copy the settings shown in **FIGURE 7.42**. The shadow is far away from the subject, very soft edged, and quite transparent.

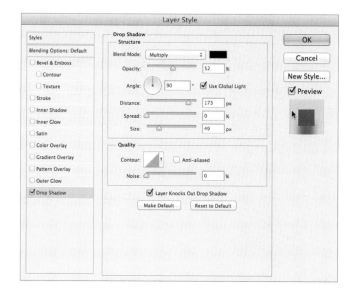

FIGURE 7.42 The Drop Shadow settings.

3. Move the playhead to the beginning of the Timeline and open the keyframe options. Because you will animate the car's position as well as the layer style, click the stopwatch for both Style and Position as shown in **FIGURE 7.43**. Yes, you can animate more than one property at a time.

FIGURE 7.43 The effect of the shadow and setting new keyframe animations.

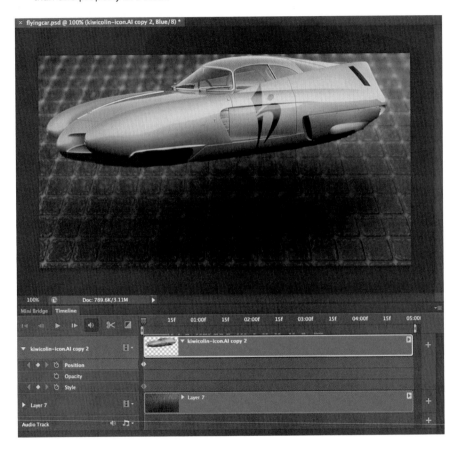

4. Move the playhead forward in time to 3 seconds as shown in **FIGURE 7.44**. Vertically reposition the car lower on the scene. With a Position Animation in place, you will make it look like it's closer to the ground by changing the shadow.

5. Double-click the word "effects" under the layer thumbnail icon in the Layers panel to open the Layer Styles dialog. Make changes to bring the shadow closer to the object, darken the shadow's opacity, and harden the edge. Follow the settings in **FIGURE 7.45**.

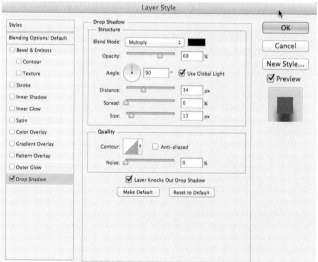

FIGURE 7.45
The settings for the closer shadow.

6. You will now see that the shadow has changed and makes it look like the car is now closer to the surface as shown in **FIGURE 7.46**.

FIGURE 7.46 The car appears closer to the surface, with harder, darker shadows.

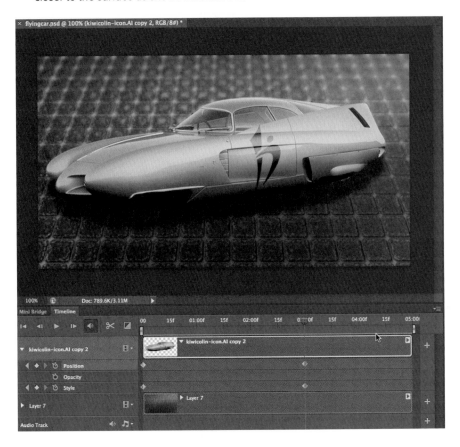

7. Play it through in the Timeline to see the result of changing the shadow (**FIGURE 4.47**). Compare your final result with the **flyingcar-shadow.psd** file in the **ch7** folder.

There are a ton more animation tricks that I would love to share with you, but space is limited and this is really a book about video. For more information on different animation effects, check out my DVD training at PhotoshopCAFE.

The next chapter covers creating animated slideshows. You will learn different ways of making things move with very little effort.

FIGURE 7.47 The shadow adds a ton of realism to this scene.

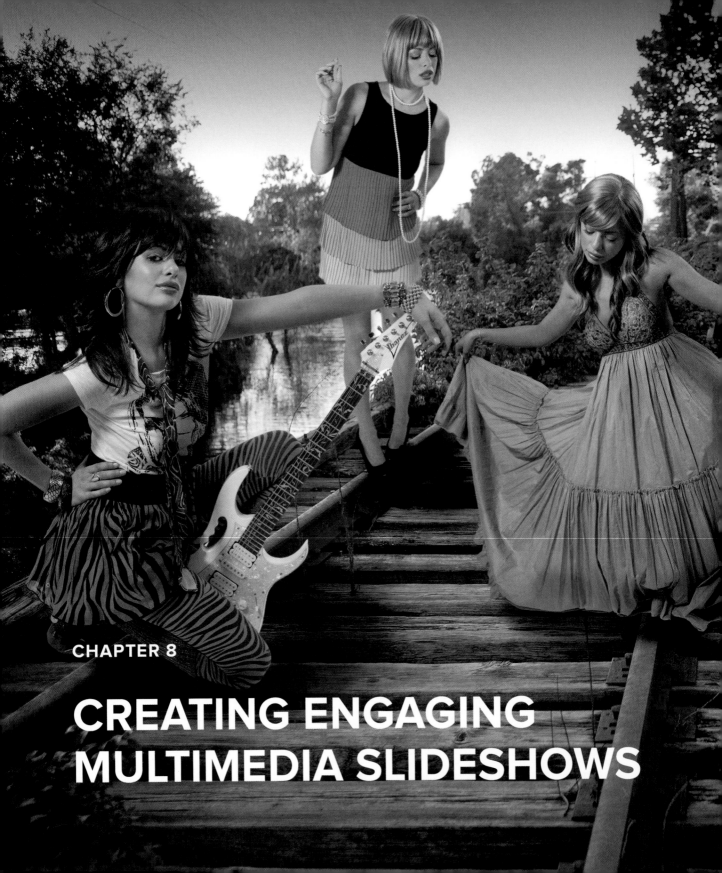

CHAPTER 8

CREATING ENGAGING MULTIMEDIA SLIDESHOWS

WHEN YOU HEAR THE TERM SLIDESHOW, what comes to mind? Do you think of a hot, dark room and the sound of a loud fan for a projector that is click-clacking away, advancing photographic slides? Maybe this is a bit too Dick Tracy for you, and your mind is more in the present. Do you think of kiosks, shop windows, tradeshows, presentations, and applications such as Microsoft PowerPoint or Apple's iMovie and Keynote? Or do you think of a documentary on the History Channel with the zoomed-in, panning images made famous by American director and producer Ken Burns? If you imagined any of these scenarios, you are correct.

The slideshow has been around a long time. It's a great way to present your photographs, ideas, and designs to clients, potential customers, and friends and family. The great thing about Photoshop slideshows is that you can mix photos, images, music, and even video all together. You can work with keyframes, make custom animations, and apply motion presets.

In this chapter, you will learn how to create awesome multimedia slideshows that include the Ken Burns effect and more. Best of all, it's easy!

Preparing Your Assets

Photographs make up the primary part of a slideshow and the first step you'll take is deciding what size to make the sideshow. The size will depend on where you plan to display it. Will it be onscreen, online, DVD? If it's going to be onscreen, find out the pixel dimensions of the screen and make your slideshow that size. In the example that follows, you're going to make a slideshow that has a screen resolution of 800px by 600px for a fictitious kiosk. It doesn't really matter what the resolution is in dots per image (DPI) or pixels per inch (PPI) as these resolutions are related to print. In multimedia playback, the only thing that matters is the screen resolution in pixels.

Now that you have decided on a slideshow size of 800 x 600, make sure your photographs are sized accordingly. Does that mean that all the images will be cropped to 800 x 600? No, unless you want a static slideshow. If you want some movement, you need to allow room for it to occur by making sure the images are large enough to accommodate the desired movement. Also, be sure that the images aren't smaller than 800 x 600, as scaling up results in a loss of quality. Finally, check that the dimensions and file sizes aren't huge, which wastes resources and can result in a loss of performance. Here are the basic requirements:

- No images smaller than the target size of the slideshow.

- For portrait orientation, the short edge (width) should be as wide as the target size.

- For zooming into an image, the image needs to be large enough to display at 100% size when fully zoomed in.

- Flattened RGB images (video is in RGB, so we want it to match the color), unless you want to animate layers separately.

TIP The bottom line is that, if at all possible, never display an image at larger than 100% magnification if you want it to look its best.

Let's dive into the project now and organize the assets.

1. If you are using the files that accompany this book, you'll find photographs to use in the **ch8/slideshow** folder. If you're using your own images, create a folder for the files you plan to use in your slideshow and give it a meaningful name.

2. Open the images in Bridge and check their sizes. You can view their sizes in the Info panel in Bridge as shown in **FIGURE 8.1**.

FIGURE 8.1 Bridge provides a quick way to see image dimensions.

3. Check all the image dimensions, and resize and crop them as necessary.

4. Make sure the images are flattened RGB files unless you want to animate elements of the images as covered later in this chapter. (I have prepared all the sample images for you.)

5. In the Folders panel, look for the name of the current folder containing the images you are reviewing in Bridge. Ctrl-click/right-click the folder name and choose Add to Favorites as shown in FIGURE 8.2. This gives you quick access to this folder in the future.

FIGURE 8.2 Creating a favorite from the working folder.

Using Mini Bridge to Place Images

Adobe Mini Bridge shares a lot of the functionality of Bridge, but it's compact and is available right inside Photoshop. For tasks such as building slideshows, it's very good.

1. Launch Mini Bridge, which is nested with the Timeline (**FIGURE 8.3**). If you don't see it at the bottom of the screen, choose > Window > Extensions > Mini Bridge.

2. At the top left of Mini Bridge, click on the menu shown in **FIGURE 8.4**. You will see that all the options are populated from Bridge. Change something in Bridge and it's reflected in Mini Bridge.

FIGURE 8.3 Mini Bridge inside of Photoshop.

FIGURE 8.4 The Mini Bridge menu.

3. Choose Favorites. Notice that the folder you added to Favorites in Bridge is available right here in Mini Bridge. In this case, I named it "slideshow book." You will see the contents of the folder in a filmstrip (**FIGURE 8.5**).

FIGURE 8.5 The contents of the selected folder in Mini Bridge.

4. Before you can add any images to the project, you need to create one. Choose File > New and create a new document with the name Slideshow and set the dimensions to 800 x 600 (FIGURE 8.6). It doesn't even matter what the background color is because you're going to delete it eventually.

FIGURE 8.6 Creating a new document.

TIP When in Mini Bridge, perhaps you are wondering how to change the size of the thumbnails. You grab the edge of the window pane and drag. As you resize Mini Bridge, it also resizes the thumbnails as shown in FIGURE 8.7.

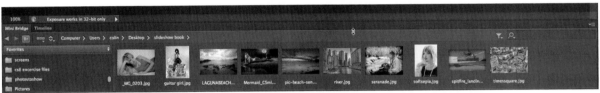

FIGURE 8.7 Resizing thumbnails in Mini Bridge.

5. With all the images visible in Mini Bridge, click the first image's thumbnail. Press Command+A (Ctrl+A) to select all the images. A border displays around them to indicate they are selected (FIGURE 8.8).

FIGURE 8.8 The folder of images all selected in Mini Bridge.

6. Here is an interesting way to add the images to the document, and it opens a cool hidden feature. Drag all the images from Mini Bridge to the document window and release the mouse button (FIGURE 8.9).

FIGURE 8.9 Dragging the images into the document window.

When you release your mouse button, you will see the first image with a bounding box around it (**FIGURE 8.10**). The image is going to be placed as a nondestructive Smart Object. This means that it can scale up and down without losing quality (provided you don't go larger than 100%).

FIGURE 8.10
Placing an image.

7. Resize the image by Shift-dragging one of the corners to constrain its shape
(**FIGURE 8.11**). If you also hold down the Option/Alt key, it will transform from the center
of the photograph. Position the photo by dragging it. Again, hold down the Shift key
to constrain the movement to the horizontal or vertical axis. When you are finished,
press the Return/Enter key and something surprising happens.

FIGURE 8.11 The resized image.

Immediately, the next image appears onscreen with bounding boxes. This is great
because it lets you work on position and size on one image at a time as shown in
FIGURE 8.12.

FIGURE 8.12 Size and position,
get into the rhythm.

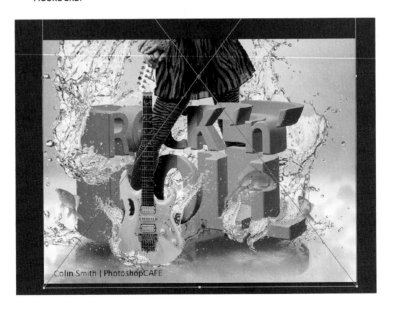

8. Size and position, press Return/Enter, size and position, press Return/Enter. See how you can get into a rhythm?

9. Keep working on all the images until they are all placed. You will notice that all the images are stacked above each other on their own respective layers. Why not use the script, Load Files into Stack? Because it doesn't allow the option to size and position each image at import.

Feel free to delete the background layer as you don't need it anymore. Your screen should now look like **FIGURE 8.13**.

TIP To stop placing images, press the Esc key. This will clear the placement clipboard. You keep the placed images, but don't have to place any more.

FIGURE 8.13 All the images are loaded as Smart Objects on layers.

Making a Slideshow

You have loaded all the images into their own stacks at this point. Now learn a great workflow and some crafty tips to quickly make a slideshow out of these images.

1. With the document open and all the images on separate layers, open the Timeline. Click the Create Video Timeline button as shown in **FIGURE 8.14**.

TIP I have come up with a workflow that you are going to love! You will only have to drag two times to get all the images into a sequence.

FIGURE 8.14 Creating a video Timeline.

A Timeline is created for each layered image as shown in **FIGURE 8.15**, but each image needs to be in a single Timeline.

FIGURE 8.15 Multiple Timelines, one for each image.

2. Slide the Timeline Magnification slider to reveal some empty space to the right of the Timeline clips. Drag the second Timeline clip and drop it after the top one as shown in **FIGURE 8.16**.

FIGURE 8.16 Dragging a clip from one Timeline to another.

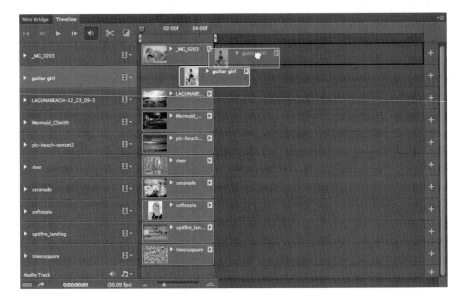

Notice what happens? A video group is automatically created with both clips nicely nested in the group (FIGURE 8.17). Remember the behavior of the video group from Chapter 4? It keeps the clips together on a single Timeline and ripples them.

3. Select all the other clips in the Layers panel by Shift-clicking the first and last clip in the list. They are all selected now as shown in FIGURE 8.18.

4. This is where it gets really good! Drag all the selected layers into the video group and release them as shown in FIGURE 8.19.

   A really beautiful thing has just happened. All the layers are now in the video group (FIGURE 8.20), but something even better has happened. All the layers are now arranged sequentially on a single Timeline (FIGURE 8.21). They are now technically a slideshow if you click the Play button. I told you that you would love this technique!

FIGURE 8.17 The Layers panel showing the new video group.

FIGURE 8.18 Selecting the additional layers.

FIGURE 8.19 Moving the layers into the video group.

FIGURE 8.20 The Layers panel arranged into a video group.

FIGURE 8.21 The Timeline showing all the images arranged into a very basic slideshow.

5. Drag the layers around in the layers stack to change their order. Remember, what is at the bottom of the Layers panel will be at the beginning of the Timeline. Finish arranging the images into the order you like (**FIGURE 8.22**). Click the Play button to make sure there are no issues. Don't worry, this is far from the end result—you are going to make things move now!

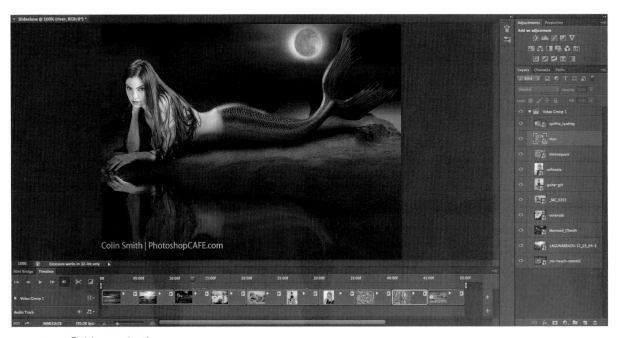

FIGURE 8.22 Finish arranging the layers so the slides play in your desired order.

FIGURE 8.23 The Motion menu.

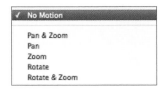

FIGURE 8.24 The five different Motion Presets available.

Adding Motion Effects to the Slideshow

Adobe has built a great slideshow tool into Photoshop. You may have noticed that the photograph clips in the Timeline are purple as opposed to blue for video. This indicates that they should be treated as graphics rather than video. The difference is apparent when you Ctrl-click/right-click a clip in the Timeline. Because there are no frames to change the speed of, nor audio to adjust, those settings would be pointless. Instead, there is a single menu called Motion Presets.

Use the Motion Presets to create a Ken Burns effect and more. Let's examine the different presets now.

1. To get started, activate the Motion Presets by choosing a purple graphics clip on the Timeline. Ctrl-click/right-click to display the menu (**FIGURE 8.23**).

2. Click the Motion menu to reveal the five different presets that are available (**FIGURE 8.24**). They are a combination of three properties: Pan, Zoom, and Rotate.

3. Read the sidebar "The Different Motion Presets for Timeline Graphics" and play around with the settings. We'll look at the Pan setting in another exercise to come.

THE DIFFERENT MOTION PRESETS FOR TIMELINE GRAPHICS

There are three types of motion available as presets and two varieties. This what they do and how to control them:

- **Pan:** Panning slides the image across the screen in any direction. It changes the position only and doesn't affect the image's scale or angular orientation. Enter a direction to pan by turning the wheel or by entering a value in the Pan field (FIGURE 8.25).

FIGURE 8.25 The Pan wheel and field.

- **Zoom:** Zoom scales the image over time. This gives the appearance of zooming in or out of the image, and offers a great way to emphasize a portion of an image. You can specify whether to zoom in or out, and from where, as shown in FIGURE 8.26. Choose Zoom In to enlarge the image over time. Choose Zoom Out to shrink the image over time. For Zoom From, click any of the nine points to set it as an anchor point that remains pinned while the rest of the image zooms. This is how you bring emphasis to a certain part of an image.

FIGURE 8.26 The Zoom controls.

- **Rotate:** The rotate behavior will cause the image to slightly spin over time. You can choose to have the slide rotate in a Clockwise or Counterclockwise direction (FIGURE 8.27).

- **Pan & Zoom:** This effect combines the Pan and Zoom behaviors and affects the slide in two ways. The image will slide across the screen while enlarging or shrinking. The options are the same as the separate Pan and Zoom controls offer (FIGURE 8.28).

- **Rotate & Zoom:** This effect combines the Pan and Rotate behaviors and affects the slide in two ways. The image will slide across the screen while enlarging or shrinking. The options are the same as the Pan and the Zoom controls together except for the orientation (FIGURE 8.29). There is no need to pick a portion of the slide, if it's already changing position.

FIGURE 8.27 The Rotate controls.

FIGURE 8.28 The Pan & Zoom controls.

FIGURE 8.29 The Rotate & Zoom effect causes the slide to spin as it zooms in or out. All the movement happens from the center of the slide.

Resizing to Fit the Canvas

You may have noticed the Resize to Fit Canvas check box with all the Motion Preset controls. This is how the toggle works.

FIGURE 8.30 shows a rotation behavior with Resize to Fit Canvas unchecked (turned off). Notice that transparency shows around the edges because the slide isn't large enough to fill the corners while being rotated. You could see how this could be a problem.

Check Resize to Fit Canvas to turn it on as shown in **FIGURE 8.31**.

FIGURE 8.30 Your "edges are showing" with Resize to Fit Canvas unchecked.

FIGURE 8.31 Turning on the Resize to Fit Canvas in the interface.

The result is really useful for slideshows. Photoshop enlarges the image as necessary to make sure it leaves no gaps as it performs its behavior, whatever that may be (**FIGURE 8.32**). This ensures nice uninterrupted slideshows without showing the edges of any slides.

FIGURE 8.32 The slides will rotate in a way that doesn't reveal any unsightly edges.

TIP Always keep Resize to Fit Canvas checked for slides. Turn it off when working with motion graphics.

Applying Motion Presets to Slides

Go through each slide and use the context menu to apply a Motion Preset to each one (Ctrl-click/right-click to display the menu). Use your discretion and experiment to see what you like best. Scrub the play head to quickly see what each effect is doing. Here is an example of one way to use the Pan preset:

1. Select the Move tool, click the slide you want to work on, and move the playhead to the beginning of the slide on the Timeline.

2. Position the slide into its beginning position as shown in FIGURE 8.33. To make things feel more natural, you will set the slide to move into position over time. It is always better for the slide to end in the desired position, not to start on it. (Of course, you can break the rules and do the opposite for a particular reaction from the audience.)

FIGURE 8.33 The slide in its starting position.

3. Choose Pan from the context menu as shown in **FIGURE 8.34**. Turn the wheel to the direction you want the slide to move. At the end, the slide will be in a nice final position. Feel free to change the position with the Move tool until you are satisfied with the move.

FIGURE 8.34 Using the Pan preset to create a motion effect.

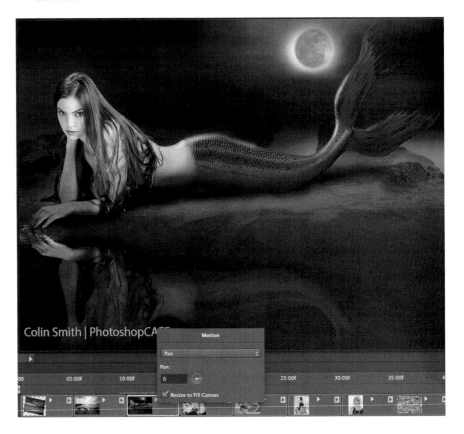

4. Continue to add Motion Presets to all the remaining slides. You will see how easy and fun they are to use.

Customizing Motion Presets

As you have already seen, Motion Presets are really easy and quick to use. The downside is that they are limited, but not as much as you think. There is a way that you can fully customize their behaviors. Maybe you want to slide farther, rotate more or less, or change the amount of zoom. You have absolute and total control over all of that. I'll show you how.

1. Using the image of the girl and the guitar as an example (**guitar girl.jpg**), select the slide and apply the Pan Motion Preset. Set the direction to −90 to move up the image. **FIGURE 8.35** shows the starting position.

FIGURE 8.35 The beginning position of the Pan movement.

At the end of the movement, notice that the image didn't move enough. It would be best to start on the word Rock 'n' Roll and pan up to show Llana's face (my model for this photograph). **FIGURE 8.36** shows the need for more movement.

FIGURE 8.36 The end of the Pan movement.

2. This is where you get into the good stuff. It's time to customize the preset. To reveal more options, click the arrow to the left of the Timeline with the video track's name. This is how you display keyframes, discussed previously in Chapter 6.

3. Move the playhead over the slide you want to customize. (You should have already applied a basic Motion Preset to it.) Click the triangle at the top middle of the slide on the Timeline. This reveals a red strip with red keyframes, indicating that a Motion Preset is applied to the clip (slide) as shown in **FIGURE 8.37**.

FIGURE 8.37 Automatic keyframes on a Motion Preset at the bottom on the clip.

4. To customize the preset, click the first keyframe. It will turn yellow to indicate that it can be changed. Move the playhead to the beginning of the clip, over the keyframe as shown in **FIGURE 8.38**.

5. Using the Move tool, reposition the image to your liking. This will be the start point of the animation. I set the image to show the words Rock 'n' Roll and the beautiful Ibanez JEM guitar that you see in **FIGURE 8.39**.

FIGURE 8.38 Select the first keyframe.

FIGURE 8.39 The new starting position of the image.

6. Select the second keyframe by clicking the diamond; it will turn yellow. Move the playhead to sit over the top of the keyframe (**FIGURE 8.40**). Notice that the keyframes are not showing as red anymore. That's because the preset motion is no longer being adjusted.

7. Reposition the end movement of the image using the Move tool. If you play the clip now, you will notice the movement has now changed to exactly what is shown in **FIGURE 8.41**. Congratulations! You have just customized your first motion preset. Let's take it further!

FIGURE 8.40 Selecting the second keyframe.

FIGURE 8.41 The ending position for the animation.

The preset was set to Pan, but now that you have customized it, you can do anything you want! How about a custom Pan along with a Zoom?

8. To zoom into Llana's face for extra impact, first select the last keyframe on the animation and set the playhead exactly on the same frame as the keyframe. Press Command+T (Ctrl+T) to select the Free Transform tool. You will see an x and adjustment nodes as shown in **FIGURE 8.42**.

FIGURE 8.42 Free transform activated on the image.

9. Grab one of the corners and Shift-drag out to scale the image up. You may need to zoom out of the canvas to give yourself more room to work and see the corner handles.

Play back the slide now and see the result of the fully customized Motion Preset in **FIGURE 8.43**. You should be starting to see the possibilities by now and ready to start playing around for yourself.

FIGURE 8.43 The custom Zoom effect added to the custom Pan effect.

Changing the Duration of Clips

If you want to make clips shorter or longer, it's easy. Place the curser at the beginning or end of the video clip, and then drag to the left or the right to extend or shorten the duration of the clip:

There are two main differences between a graphics clip and a video clip when changing the duration.

■ You can extend the length of a graphics clip as long as you like; the length is not limited to captured footage like a video clip.

■ You won't see a preview window with a graphics clip like you do with a video clip.

Creating a Title Slide

A great thing about slideshows in Photoshop is that they aren't limited to photos and static images. For example, you can also add an animated title screen. Follow these steps to build the screen and insert it into the slideshow:

1. Begin by opening the base title screen I have prepared for you. Open **title screen.psd** from the **ch8**/**title screen** folder. It's an image with two text blocks as shown in **FIGURE 8.44**.

2. Make sure the Timeline is visible and click the Create Video Timeline button as shown in **FIGURE 8.45**.

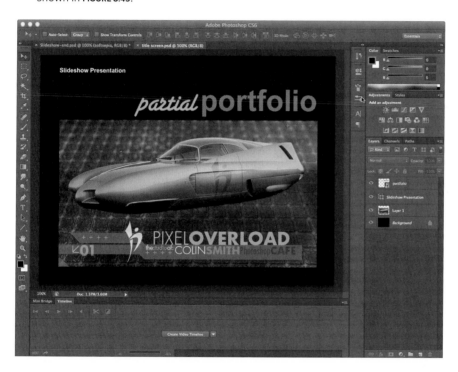

FIGURE 8.44 The beginning title screen.

FIGURE 8.45 The Create Video Timeline button turns the image into a layered animation.

3. Drag the end of each track in the Timeline to shorten the length of the slide to 4 seconds as shown in **FIGURE 8.46**.

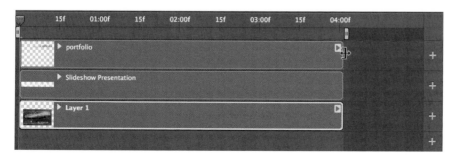

FIGURE 8.46 Changing the duration of the video tracks.

FIGURE 8.47 Converting the Background into a regular layer.

FIGURE 8.48 Adjusting the length of a track in the Timeline panel.

4. Notice that the black background didn't get converted to a Timeline track; that's because it's a locked background layer. To fix this, hold down the Option/Alt key and double-click the Padlock icon in the Layer panel as shown in **FIGURE 8.47**. It's now converted to a regular layer, and it automatically gets added to the Timeline.

5. Drag the end of the video clip in the Timeline to shorten the length of the black background layer. Everything is now set up for adding the animation as shown in **FIGURE 8.48**.

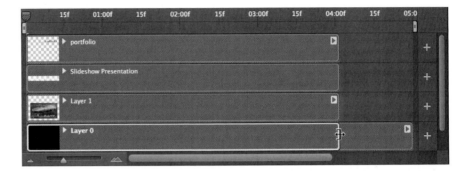

6. Hide the top two text layers in the Layers panel (one is a Smart Object and the other is a vector shape). Select Layer 1, the image layer, as shown in **FIGURE 8.49**.

7. To fade this layer in over time, move the playhead to 1 second. Click the disclosure triangle to the left of the Layer 1 track name in the Timeline. This opens the key-frame options. Click the stopwatch to the left of Opacity as shown in **FIGURE 8.50**. There is now a keyframe at 1 second.

FIGURE 8.49 The layer panel with the top two layers hidden.

FIGURE 8.50 Setting an Opacity keyframe.

8. Drag the playhead back to the beginning of the Timeline (**FIGURE 8.51**). In the Layers panel, change the Opacity on the selected Layer 1 to 0. This will create a nice fade-in of the slide. Go ahead and test it.

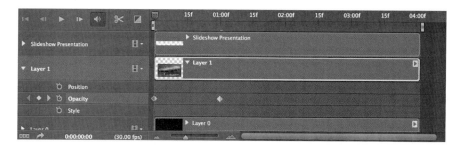

FIGURE 8.51 Finishing the fade effect on the Timeline.

9. It's time to animate the text now. Move the playhead to 1 second. In the Layers panel, turn on the visibility of the two text layers by clicking the box to the left of their Layer thumbnails. An eye icon will show to indicate layer visibility is on as shown in **FIGURE 8.52**.

FIGURE 8.52 Turning on layer visibility.

10. Click the triangle next to the text layers, Portfolio and Slideshow Presentation. Add a keyframe by clicking the stopwatch to the left of Transform on the Portfolio layer. On the Slideshow Presentation layer, if you try to animate the Position property, you will get a warning message and nothing will happen. You can't directly animate the position of a vector shape. What you need to do is scroll down the list of properties in the Timeline until you see the Vector Mask Position option. Click the stopwatch to add a keyframe. To animate a vector shape, you must animate its Vector Mask, not its position. **FIGURE 8.53** shows the added keyframes.

FIGURE 8.53 Setting keyframes for Transform and Vector Mask position and working on two video layers at the same time.

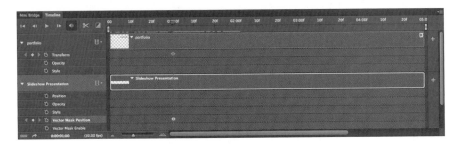

11. Now, to animate the text layers, move the playhead to the first frame on the Timeline. Select the top text layer, Portfolio. Shift-drag the text to the right until it's positioned slightly off the screen (Shift constrains the movement to horizontal or vertical) as shown in **FIGURE 8.54**. Select the new text layer, Slideshow Presentation, hold down the Shift key, and drag to the left to position it slightly off the screen.

FIGURE 8.54 Preparing the text layers for their animation.

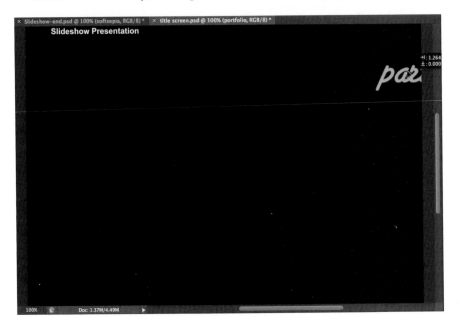

12. Now, play back the animation. Notice that the animations play back perfectly. If not, go back and follow the steps again or troubleshoot to see where you went wrong. Open **title-screen done.psd** from the **ch8**/**title screen** folder to see the final result as shown in **FIGURE 8.55**.

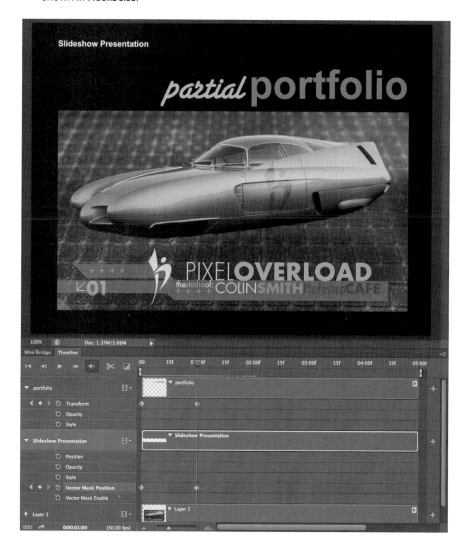

FIGURE 8.55 The title slide animation is now complete.

FIGURE 8.56 Nesting the title slide into a single Smart Object.

FIGURE 8.57 Dragging the Smart Object into another document to combine animations.

Combining Different Animations

You have just finished creating an animated title screen for your slideshow in progress. So the question may arise: How do you take the animated title screen and add it to the slideshow? It's actually quite easy. Here are the steps:

1. Open the file **title screen-done.psd**, (if it's not already open) from the **ch8/title screen** folder. You'll prepare the title screen for moving by selecting all the layers in the Layers panel and Ctrl-clicking/right-clicking the top layer name and choosing the Convert to Smart Object option. The entire title screen is now nested as a single Smart Object as shown in **FIGURE 8.56**.

2. Open the **slideshow-done.psd** file. Make sure the playhead is on the first frame and all the keyframe disclosures are collapsed. The document is now ready to receive the slide. Click the top tab in Photoshop to open the Slideshow document again. Make sure the slide is selected in the Layers panel. Hold down the Shift key and drag from the center of the slideshow onscreen all the way up to the tab for the slideshow as shown in **FIGURE 8.57**.

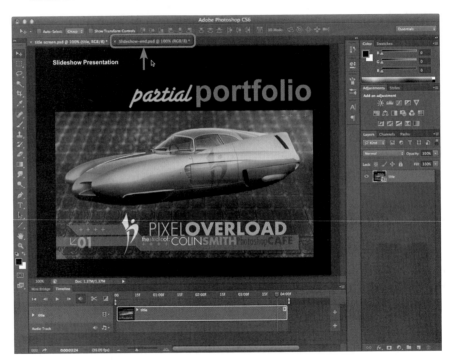

3. When the window changes to the slideshow, drag down into the document and release. You should see a new video track with the title on it. **FIGURE 8.58** demonstrates this.

FIGURE 8.58 The added clip on its own video layer.

4. Drag the title clip to the beginning of the slideshow video track. It will drop into the beginning and all the other clips will nudge to the right as shown in **FIGURE 8.59**. The extra video track will disappear from the top because there is nothing in it. All the pieces should now be in place.

FIGURE 8.59 Moving the clip to a different video layer to add it to the Timeline.

5. As a finishing touch for this part of the slideshow, add some transitions (**FIGURE 8.60**). (If you need a refresher on transitions, go back to Chapter 4.) Set the Transition Time to 2 seconds. Drag a Cross Fade between each slide and drop a Fade to Black on the end. You don't technically need a Fade to Black at the beginning because the slide is animated. However, adding a Fade from Black at the start will cause the text to fade in as it moves. I added a fade on the sample image, but its use is totally your call. To see the project so far, open the **slideshow-transitions.psd** file from the **ch8** folder and play through it. The animation should be looking pretty good at this point!

FIGURE 8.60 Adding transitions to complete the slide.

Adding Music to a Slideshow

The slideshow is looking really good at this point. For full impact, it just needs music, which is very easy to add. For this exercise, you will use an original score by Michael Burns, the song "Rescue Me," with permission. This is one of the many royalty-free, licensed tracks available through triplescoopmusic.com, a great source for finding quality music to bolster your productions.

 TIP Chapter 5 covers audio in greater detail.

 TIP If you prefer, use one of your own music tracks. Just remember to respect copyrights—it's not just a good idea and ethical, it's the law and you could get in trouble for using music you don't have permission to use.

1. In the bottom of the Timeline, click by the music notes on the Audio Track. When the menu displays, select Add Audio as shown in **FIGURE 8.61**.

2. Navigate to your download folder and choose the **music** folder to find the **michaelburns_rescuemeinstrumental.mp3** track as shown in **FIGURE 8.62**.

3. The music track is added in green. Zoom out of the Timeline to see the full music track. Drag from the end and make it the same length as the rest of the animation as shown in **FIGURE 8.63**.

FIGURE 8.61
Adding an audio track.

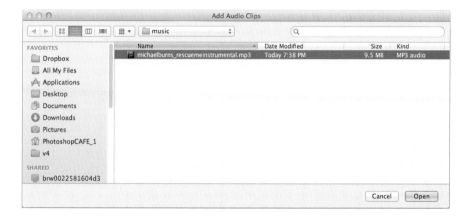

FIGURE 8.62 Choosing an mp3 file to add as a music track.

4. Ctrl-click/right-click the audio track and adjust the options. Set 2 seconds of fade out, so the music slowly fades to silence at the end of the animation as shown in **FIGURE 8.64**. You don't need to fade it in, because the song starts naturally. If you start playing partway into the song, then a 2 second fade in would probably work well. Also, adjust the overall volume of the music if it's too loud.

FIGURE 8.63 Adjusting the length of the music track.

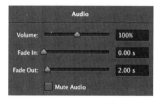

Now that the slideshow is complete, it's time to share it with the world. I hope you take these principles and create your own slideshow, featuring, well, you! Create a slideshow that shows off your photography and artistic genius.

FIGURE 8.64 Making some final adjustments to the music track.

The slideshow will be exported as a video file. It can be uploaded to YouTube or Facebook, or played back on your favorite computer or mobile device.

The next chapter walks you through the process of outputting your video. Don't worry—it's much easier than you think.

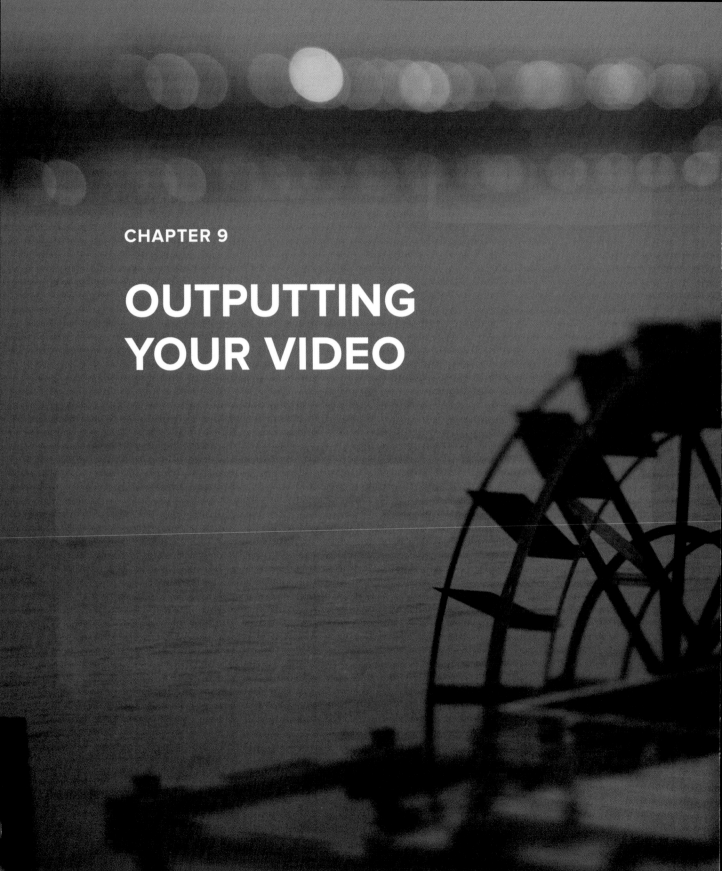

CHAPTER 9

OUTPUTTING YOUR VIDEO

VIDEO THAT IS SITTING ON YOUR COMPUTER may be fun for you to watch, but the goal is to get it out to the world! You may want to upload a video to YouTube or Vimeo, so that anyone or a select group of people can see it online. Or, you might want to share it on social networks such as Facebook or Twitter. Perhaps you would like to present your creation in person on a laptop, tablet device, or smartphone. Maybe you just want to do some motion graphics in Photoshop and then continue editing in a program such as Adobe Premiere Pro or Apple Final Cut Pro. No matter what your goal is, this chapter shows you how to get your creation out of Photoshop and into a format that can be viewed and shared.

Rendering Video

When a Photoshop project is ready for use—whether for viewing or editing in another application—the video needs to be rendered. The rendering process is where the project becomes video by converting the Timeline frames to video frames. It doesn't matter if you have edited a video or created a slideshow, motion graphics, or animated 3D. Anything that is animated needs to be rendered to video.

To render video, either click the arrow button ➡ in the lower-left corner of the Timeline or use the File > Export > Render Video menu command as shown in **FIGURE 9.1**.

FIGURE 9.1 Choosing File > Export > Render Video to output a video.

Customizing the Render Settings

The Render Video dialog is shown in **FIGURE 9.2**. The most common options, Location and Range, are detailed here.

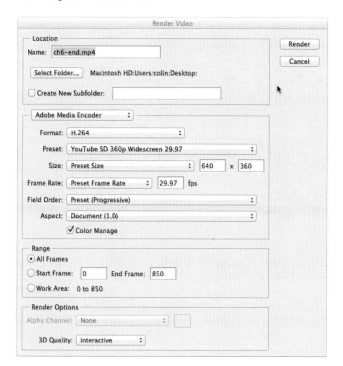

FIGURE 9.2
The Render Video dialog.

Specifying a location

Controls in the Location area specify the name and location for the rendered video file.

- **Name:** Enter a meaningful name for the rendered video.

- **Select Folder:** Specify a location for the rendered video file.

- **Create New Subfolder:** Create a new subfolder at the selected location if it will make it easier for you to find the video later.

Selecting a range

The range is where you decide how much of the Timeline gets rendered. At first, render only a few seconds of the project. This way, you can test the video without having to wait for the entire thing to render. It's common to experiment with a few different output options to get the best quality at the smallest size. Once you are happy with the result, then and only then should you render the whole video. The Range options work as follows:

- **All Frames:** This first setting, the self-explanatory default, will render the entire Timeline to video.

- **Start Frame/End Frame:** Change the Start Frame and End Frame if you want to render a single frame or ranges of frames. This is often used with the Image Sequence option (covered later in this chapter).

- **Work Area:** If you want to render a work area specified on the Timeline, click this option. A work area is a snapshot of the Timeline. Some people like to assemble their videos on the Timeline, but define a working area as their "canvas." Others use a portion of the Timeline as a work area, to refine a specific section of the video, maybe refine a cut or move. If there is a specific Work Area set, it will show up in the Frame numbers in the Render menu.

Setting the work area on the Timeline

By default, the work area is the entire contents of the Timeline as defined by gray brackets at each end. To choose a work area, drag the gray bars and notice that the active work area is a different shade of gray than the unselected portion. **FIGURE 9.3** shows a work area defined. To move the entire work area, select between the gray brackets and slide the entire region to the left or right.

FIGURE 9.3 A work area defined by dragging the gray brackets.

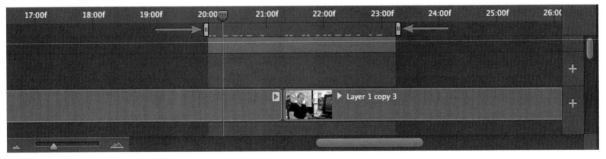

Rendering Video for Consumption

Rendering for consumption means rendering video for people to watch. It's very easy to do this thanks to a robust set of presets, which are predefined output settings. For the majority of rendering, this is where you are going to go.

1. In the Render Video dialog (File > Export > Render Video), specify a name and location for the rendered video file.

2. Choose Adobe Media Encoder (the default) from the menu.

   Leave the Format set to H.264 (the default) as shown in **FIGURE 9.4**.

3. Choose an option from the Preset menu shown in **FIGURE 9.5**. As you can see, preset options range from Android Phones and Tablets to Apple Phones and Tablets, from Apple TV to HD and SD video formats, and from Vimeo to YouTube. To use the working document size and frame rate, choose High, Medium, or Low Quality.

■ To present the video on a mobile device, choose a preset for a mobile device such as Android Phone & Tablet or Apple TV, iPad, iPhone.

■ To upload to the web for viewing on the Internet, choose from the Vimeo or YouTube presets. Don't choose a preset that is larger than your video size or loss of quality will occur. Note that these online services also run their own compression when a video is uploaded.

When you choose a preset, the video will be resized so that it looks the best on the target device. If the aspect ratio is different, black bars will be added to the sides or top and bottom, which is preferable to the video being stretched or squashed.

TIP H.264, the most common video format used today, provides high-quality video at small file sizes. Most cameras and other video devices shoot in H.264. It's used on just about every mobile device, the web, Vimeo, and YouTube. Even Adobe Flash can play H.264 format natively through the Flash player. Blu-ray Discs play H.264 as do devices such as Sony Playstations.

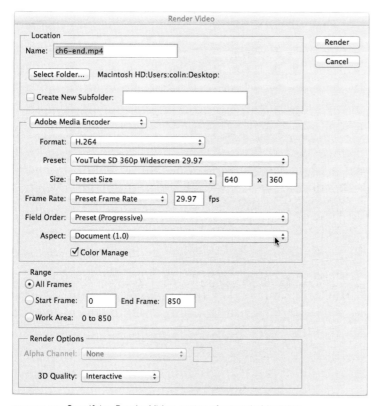

FIGURE 9.4 Specifying Render Video settings for watchable video.

FIGURE 9.5 Choosing a preset for rendering the video.

4. Click OK, and wait for the video or slideshow to be rendered out to disk.

Once the video is rendered, you can upload the file to your website, mobile device, or favorite social network; you can copy it to a disk, thumbdrive, DVD, or dropbox; and you can send it as an email attachment.

CUSTOM VIDEO SETTINGS

You can specify some settings manually for a custom size, for example. Choose Quick-Time as the format and then under the Size menu, choose Custom. Most of the time, however, you can skip the settings and just choose a preset, which includes all the settings needed to render the video correctly.

- **Size:** This is the output size the video will render to. Choose standard sizes from the menu or enter a custom size.

- **Frame Rate:** This specifies how many frames of video will display each second. Choose common frame rates or enter a frame rate value in the field.

- **Field Order:** This is where you choose Upper or Lower for interlaced video. Interlaced video is an old-fashioned way of reducing video bandwidth by half as you would see on an old tube TV. The horizontal lines are interlacing. Half the video is shown at a time. Video is split into Upper or Lower Fields, referring to which set of lines play at a time. These fields alternate or cycle so quickly that the eye sees the entire picture at once. I suggest choosing the progressive for the best-looking video unless you need to deliver it as interlaced for an older standard. If that's the case, try out both Upper and Lower and choose the one that looks the best.

    In modern video, you will use progressive compression, which is noninterlaced and relies on image compression to reduce file size. Interlaced is pretty much obsolete, although it's still around on some footage.

- **Aspect:** This is where you choose different pixel aspect ratios. If the image appears too skinny or too fat, change the aspect ratio. This was discussed in more detail in Chapter 1, "Shooting Video: The Basics of Video Production."

Higher-Quality Encoding

If you need higher-quality video, that includes more information and more options beyond H.264, you will need to use higher-quality encoding options. For example, maybe you are using Photoshop to create motion graphics or animated 3D, but you need to continue work in an application such as After Effects or Adobe Premiere Pro. This section covers *working formats* rather than *delivery formats,* so the emphasis is on high quality over file size.

Exporting Uncompressed Video

To render the highest quality of a cut sequence or slideshow for work in another NLE (nonlinear editing program), you need to export uncompressed video.

1. Set the Render Video options as specified earlier in this chapter.

2. Choose QuickTime from the Format menu rather than H.264 (**FIGURE 9.6**).

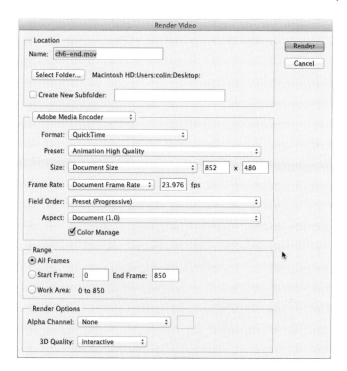

FIGURE 9.6
Rendering uncompressed video.

TIP At the time of this writing, you cannot open a Photoshop Timeline in Adobe Premiere Pro and use it that way. (You can import the .psd, but the video won't play back.) The solution is to render everything as QuickTime video first, so you can work with the resulting video clip in another application.

3. Choose either Animation High Quality or Uncompressed. (I prefer Animation High Quality because of its transparency support as discussed later in this section.)

4. To preserve the best quality, leave the document size as is unless you have a reason to customize it.

5. Click Render. Don't be alarmed if the file size is huge—this is the cost of exporting the highest possible quality.

Rendering Transparency

TIP You can render out transparency with an image sequence also, by choosing a format that supports transparency such as PSD or TIFF (image sequences are covered in the next section). The remaining steps are the same as below.

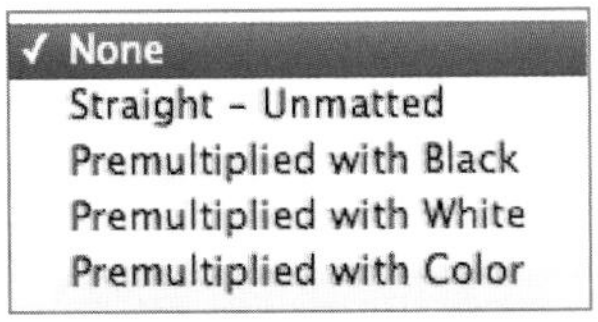

Sometimes, you will need to render video with transparency. Usually, it's because you have created an overlay graphic that you want to include on another video composition. It might be back here in Photoshop, in After Effects, or in Adobe Premiere Pro. Maybe you are creating a lower third or a callout graphic. If you're animating any 3D object to be displayed over transparency, you will also want to take note. There is only one way to render out a video with transparency from Photoshop.

1. In the Render Video dialog (File > Export > Render Video) choose QuickTime from the Format menu and Animation for the preset.

2. When Animation is selected, the Alpha Channel menu becomes available in the Render Options area at the bottom of the dialog. The Alpha Channel menu, shown in **FIGURE 9.7**, offers the same options as After Effects. Choose an option as follows:

FIGURE 9.7 Transparency options.

- **None:** Produces no transparency as shown in **FIGURE 9.8**. Use this setting when there are no transparent portions of the video.

- **Straight – Unmatted:** Creates transparency without a matte edge as shown in **FIGURE 9.9**. This option works best when the video will be used against different types of colored backgrounds or high-contrast backdrops. The edges could appear a little jaggy, but most of the time video exported with this option looks great.

- **Premultiplied with Black:** This option creates a smooth, antialiased edge that blends with a black fringe as shown in **FIGURE 9.10**. It produces very smooth edges when placed against a black backdrop.

FIGURE 9.8 Use None for a white background with no transparency.

- **Premultiplied with White:** This option creates a smooth, antialiased edge that blends with a white fringe as shown in **FIGURE 9.11**. It produces very smooth edges when placed against a white backdrop.

- **Premultiplied with Color:** This option creates a smooth, antialiased edge that blends with the colored fringe you choose from a color swatch that appears as shown in **FIGURE 9.12**. It produces very smooth edges when placed against a backdrop of a consistent color.

3. Click Render.

FIGURE 9.9 Use Straight - Unmatted for a transparency without a matte edge.

FIGURE 9.10 When using Premultiplied with Black, notice that the dark edges will look great against black.

FIGURE 9.11 When using Premultiplied with White, notice how the edges blend in perfectly with the white page here.

FIGURE 9.12 Using Premultiplied with Color looks great against the same colored solid background.

Selecting an Image Sequence

At times, you will want to export an image sequence rather than video. The difference is an image sequence renders each frame out as an individual image. A 200-frame video would be exported as 200 individual images, each one showing a progression of movement. Image sequences are most commonly used for visual effects. To render an image sequence, follow these steps:

1. In the Render Video dialog, choose Photoshop Image Sequence from the Adobe Media Encoder menu (**FIGURE 9.13**).

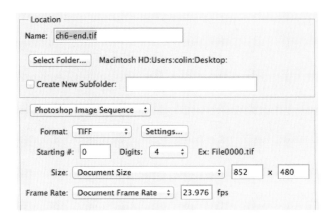

FIGURE 9.13

Choosing an image sequence type in the Render Video dialog.

2. Choose an option from the Format menu for the individual image files. Formats such as JPG and TIFF have compression options. Click the Settings button to customize those options. For details on the image compression options, consult the Photoshop Help file.

3. For the Frame Rate, which determines how many images are created for each second of video, specify the frame rate of the target project. If you don't know, then the Document Frame Rate option yields the best results.

4. Specify a Starting Frame (unless you are using a custom range as described above). Set the amount of digits to create leading zeros based on how many frames are to be converted to images. This will keep the images sorted in the correct order when working with the sequence later as 002 is listed before 010, but 10 would be listed before 2.

5. Specify a location for the rendered files and create a subfolder to help keep them all together.

6. Click Render and Photoshop will go to work.

Working with 3D

If you want to create 3D animation from Photoshop, you will need to have Photoshop Extended version. A common workflow is to animate the 3D and then bring it into After Effects and composite there. Because After Effects CS6 doesn't support 3D directly within the program, you can no longer place a 3D object from Photoshop into After Effects. When rendering out 3D, save as Animation and choose a transparent matte if there is any transparency in the animation.

While this book doesn't cover 3D, I wanted to give you just a quick rundown of some of the settings and what they mean.

At the bottom of the Render Video dialog in the Render Options is the 3D Quality menu. There are three options as shown in **FIGURE 9.14**.

- **Interactive:** This is the best option for testing as it offers the fastest rendering time by skipping things like reflection. Use this for timing and placement.

- **Ray Traced Draft:** Use this option when you are happy with the timing and everything looks good as far as movement. Ray Traced Draft produces a decent render that is good for reviewing, getting client approval, and proofing.

- **Ray Traced Final:** When you have the final approval from your client, or you like everything yourself and there are no more changes, then it's time for the Ray Traced Final. This will produce the best possible rendering result from Photoshop, but be warned, it takes a long time to render an animation. This is the kind of task you will want to start before going to bed at night or heading out the door. You don't want to sit and stare at the screen—it can take hours or even days for the computer to render a complex animation.

FIGURE 9.14
Options shown for 3D.

TIP To change the Ray Tracing settings, go to Photoshop > Preferences > 3D. On Windows, it's Edit > Preferences > 3D. The main setting you will change is the High Quality Threshold. Each number represents a pass of the renderer over the frame, and the image quality improves with each pass. Experiment and find the lowest number that will work for you because, remember, Photoshop is going to produce all of these passes on each frame and each pass can take a while if there are soft shadows, transparency, and reflections in the scene. Then there are 24 or 30 frames for each second of animation. I think you get the idea.

Conclusion

Thank you for buying this book and reading it. I hope I have provided the building blocks you need to experiment and see what's possible with Photoshop video and animation.

I'm really hoping that I have inspired you to work more with video. I would love to see your creations and be happy to answer any questions. I can always be found on all the social networks as kiwicolin or PhotoshopCAFE or hanging out in the forums at PhotoshopCAFE.com. You can also contact me through the wonderful people at Peachpit Press (ask@peachpit.com).

Happy editing!

Colin

INDEX